DID THE GREEKS GREEKS BELIEVE IN THEIR MYTHS?

Paul Veyne
Translated by
Paula Wissing

The University of Chicago Press

Chicago and London

DID THE GREEKS BELIEVE IN THEIR MYTHS?

An Essay on
the Constitutive Imagination

PAUL VEYNE is professor of Roman history at the University of Paris (Collège de France). A leading intellectual in France, where he is best known for his study of aristocratic power in ancient Greece and Rome, *Le pain et le cirque,* he is an editor of and contributor to *A History of Private Life.* His *Roman Erotic Elegy: Love, Poetry, and the West* is also published by the University of Chicago Press.

Originally published as *Les Grecs ont-ils cru à leurs mythes?*
© Editions du Seuil, 1983.

The University of Chicago Press, Chicago 60637
The University of Chicago Press, Ltd., London

97 96 95 94 93 92 91 90   5 4 3

Library of Congress Cataloging-in-Publication Data

Veyne, Paul, 1930–
   Did the Greeks believe in their myths?

   Translation of: Les Grecs ont-ils cru à leurs mythes?
   Bibliography: p. 131.
   Includes index.
   1. Mythology, Greek.   I. Title.
BL782.V4713   1988   292'.13   87–25536
ISBN 0–226–85433–7
ISBN 0–226–85434–5 (pbk.)

To Estelle Blanc

. . . Que um conjunto real e verdadeiro
é uma doença das nossas ideias.

Pessoa

Contents

Translator's Note

I have made every attempt to keep as close to the original text as possible and at the same time convey something of the grace and fluidity of the author's style. Two specific points should be brought to the reader's attention. In allusions to the works of classical and neoclassical writers, the names of the gods and heroes have been given in the form that the writer cited would have used (e.g., Aphrodite in Pausanias, but Venus in Cicero). Since French writers of the Renaissance and the neoclassical period tended to use the Roman forms of these names, even in works dealing with Greek subjects, that practice has been adhered to. Also, I have occasionally used the somewhat gothic-sounding term ''supernatural'' as a gloss to the French *merveilleux* or *le merveilleux*. Although supernatural is perhaps not the best term to associate with Greek attitudes toward mythology, the context of the author's discussions sometimes made the use of other less surprising terms (''marvelous,'' ''fabulous,'' etc.) confusing. The author also uses the term *surnaturel*—rarely, to be sure—but again to refer to the realm of myth and legend as opposed to everyday reality. I hope that the more frequent use of the term does not distort his thought.

Preface

How is it possible to half-believe, or believe in contradictory things? Children believe that Santa Claus comes down the chimney, bringing them toys, and at the same time believe that these toys are put there by their parents. Do they then really believe in Santa Claus? Yes, and the faith of the Dorzé is no less whole. In the eyes of these Ethiopians, says Dan Sperber, "the leopard is a Christian animal who respects the fasts of the Coptic church, the observance of which, in Ethiopia, is the principal test of religion. Nonetheless, a Dorzé is no less careful to protect his livestock on Wednesdays and Fridays, the fast days, than on other days of the week. He holds it true that leopards fast and that they eat every day. Leopards are dangerous every day; this he knows by experience. They are Christian; tradition proves it."

Taking the example of the Greek belief in their myths, I have set out to study the plurality of the modalities of belief—belief based on word, on experience, and so on. This examination has led me somewhat further on two occasions.

It was necessary to recognize that, instead of speaking of beliefs, one must actually speak of truths, and that these truths were themselves products of the imagination. We are not creating a false idea of things. It is the truth of things that through the centuries has been so oddly constituted. Far from being the most simple realistic experience, truth is the most historical. There was a time when poets and historians invented royal dynasties all of a piece, complete with the name of each potentate and his genealogy. They were not forgers, nor were they acting in bad faith. They were simply following what was, at the time, the normal way of arriving at the truth. If we take this idea to its conclusion, we see that we hold true, in this same way, what we would call fiction after we have put down the book. The *Iliad* and *Alice in Wonderland* are no less true than Fustel de Coulanges.

Similarly, we look on the totality of the past as dreams, certainly interesting ones, and regard only the latest state of science as true, and that only provisionally so. This is culture.

I do not at all mean to say that the imagination will bring future truths to light and that it should reign; I mean, rather, that truths are already products of the imagination and that the imagination has always governed. It is imagination that rules, not reality, reason, or the ongoing work of the negative.

This imagination is not the faculty we know psychologically and historically by the same name. It does not, through dream or prophecy, expand the fishbowl in which we live. On the contrary, it creates boundaries. Outside this bowl is nothing, not even future truths. We cannot make them speak. Religions and literatures, as well as politics, modes of conduct, and sciences are formed within these containers. This imagination is a faculty, but in the Kantian sense of the word. It is transcendental; it creates our world instead of providing the leavening or being the demon. However—and this would make any Kantian worthy of the name faint with horror—this transcendence is historical; for cultures succeed one another, and each one is different. Men do not find the truth; they create it, as they create their history. And the two in turn offer a good return.

My cordial thanks to Michel Foucault, with whom I discussed this book; to my colleagues at the Association of Greek Studies, Jacques Bompaire and Jean Bousquet; and to François Wahl, for his suggestions and criticisms.

Introduction

Did the Greeks believe in their mythology? The answer is difficult, for "believe" means so many things. Not everyone believed that Minos, after his death, continued being a judge in Hell[1] or that Theseus fought the Minotaur,[2] and they knew that poets "lie." However, their way of not believing these things is disturbing to us. For in the minds of the Greeks, Theseus had, nonetheless, existed. It was necessary only to "purify Myth by Reason"[3] and refine the biography of Heracles' companion to its historic nugget. As for Minos, Thucydides, at the cost of prodigious mental effort, uncovers the same core at the heart of this subject: "Of all those we know by hearsay, Minos was the earliest to have a navy."[4] Phaedra's father, the husband of Pasiphaë, is no more than a king who was master of the sea. The purification of myth by *logos* is not another episode in the eternal struggle between superstition and reason, dating from earliest times to the days of Voltaire and Renan, which would bring glory to the Greek spirit. Despite Nestle, myth and *logos* are not opposites, like truth and error.[5] Myth was a subject of serious reflection,[6] and the Greeks still had not tired of it six hundred years after the movement of the Sophists, which we have called their *Aufklärung*. Far from being a triumph of reason, the purification of myth by *logos* is an ancient program whose absurdity surprises us today. Why did the Greeks go to the trouble of wishing to separate the wheat from the chaff in myth when they could easily have rejected both Theseus and the Minotaur, as well as the very existence of a certain Minos and the improbable stories tradition gave him? We see the extent of the problem when we realize that this attitude toward myth lasted for over two millennia. In a history in which the truths of the Christian religion and the realities of the past lend support to each other, the *Discours sur l'histoire universelle,* Bossuet combines mythological chronology with the

1

sacred chronology of the world since creation. In this way he is able to date "the famous battles of Hercules, son of Amphitryon," and the death of "Sarpedon, the son of Jupiter," a "short time after Abimilech."[7] What did the bishop of Meaux have in mind when he wrote this? What is going on in our minds when we believe contradictory things, as we constantly do in matters of politics or on the subject of psychoanalysis?

We are in much the same position as a folklorist faced with a treasure trove of legends or Freud pondering Schreber's logorrhea. What is to be made of this mass of nonsense? How can all this not have a meaning, a motivation, a function, or at least a structure? The question of whether myths have an authentic content can never be put in positive terms. To know whether Minos ever existed, we must first of all decide whether myths are simply hollow tales or whether they are altered history. No positivist criticism can adequately deal with mythology and the supernatural.[8] Then how does it happen that people cease believing in legends? How did people come to stop believing in Theseus, the founder of Athenian democracy, in Romulus, the founder of Rome, or in the historicity of the first centuries of Roman history? What made them no longer believe in the Trojan origins of the Frankish monarchy?

Thanks to George Huppert's fine book on Estienne Pasquier, we have a clearer idea about the modern era.[9] History as we know it was born, not when criticism was invented—for that happened long ago—but on the day when the work of the critic and the work of the historian were joined in one task: "Historical research was practiced for many centuries without seriously affecting the way of writing history, the two activities remaining foreign to each other, sometimes in the mind of the same man." Was the same thing true in Antiquity? Does historical reasoning follow a royal road, the same in each period? We will take as our guiding thread an idea of A. D. Momigliano: "Modern methods of historical research are completely founded on the distinction between original and secondary sources."[10] It is not altogether certain that this great scholar's idea is correct; I believe that it is not even pertinent. But it has the merit of presenting, albeit in the form of an opposition, a methodological problem, and it has appearances in its favor. Think of Beaufort or Niebuhr, whose skepticism concerning the early centuries of Roman history was founded on the absence of contemporary sources and documents from these distant ages or was at least justified by this absence.[11]

The history of the sciences is not the story of the progressive discovery of good methods and true truths. The Greeks have their own way of believing in their mythology or being skeptical of it, and their way only appears to resemble our own. They also have their way of writing history, which is not our way. The Greek way relies on an implicit presupposition of such a kind that the distinction between original and secondary sources, far from being ignored out of methodological weakness, is simply irrelevant. Pausanias provides an excellent example of this way, and we will refer to him often.

Pausanias is not a mind to be underestimated, and we do him an injustice when we accept the assessment of his *Description of Greece* as the Baedeker of ancient Greece. Pausanias is the equal of any of the great nineteenth-century German philologists or philosophers. To describe the monuments and narrate the history of the different countries of Greece, he combed the libraries, traveled a great deal, cultivated himself, and saw it all with his own eyes.[12] He approaches collecting local oral legends with the zeal of a French provincial scholar of the days of Napoleon III. The precision of his descriptions and the breadth of his knowledge are astounding. He amazes us, too, by his visual accuracy (by examining sculpture and inquiring about dates, Pausanias learned to date statuary according to stylistic criteria). And, as we will see, Pausanias was obsessed by the problem of myth and wrestled with this enigma.

1
When Historical Truth Was Tradition and Vulgate

There is a good reason why the ancient historians rarely offer us the opportunity to ascertain whether they make a distinction between primary and secondary sources. A historian of this period does not cite his sources or, rather, he does so rarely, irregularly, and not at all for the same reasons as we do. If we seek to understand the implications of this silence and pursue the consequences, the whole picture will emerge. We will see that history then and history now are alike in name only. Not that history then was imperfect and had only to progress to fully become the Science it would then forever be. In its own genre, ancient history was as complete a means of creating belief as our journalism of today, which it resembles a great deal. This "hidden part of the iceberg" of what history was, long ago, is so immense that . . . we realize that it is not the same iceberg.

The ancient historian does not use footnotes. Whether he does original research or works from secondary sources, he wishes to be taken at his word—unless he is proud of having discovered a little-known author or wants to bring to public attention a rare and precious text, which to him is in this case a kind of monument rather than a source.[13] Most often Pausanias is content to say, "I learned that . . . ", or "According to my informants . . . ." These informants, or exegetes,* may be written documents or information collected orally from the priests or local scholars he encountered during his travels.[14] This silence concerning sources has not ceased to puzzle us and has given rise to the *Quellenforschung*.

Let us return to Estienne Pasquier, whose *Recherches de la France* appeared in 1560. Before publishing it, G. Huppert tells us, Pasquier circulated his manuscript among his friends.[15] Their most frequent reproach concerned Pasquier's habit of giving too many references to the sources he cited. This procedure, they told him, cast a "scholastic pall'' (''umbre des escholes'') on the book and was unbecoming in a work of history. Was it truly necessary each time to confirm his ''words by some ancient author''? If it was a matter of lending his account authority and credibility, time alone would see to that. After all, the works of the Ancients were not encumbered by citations, and their authority had been affirmed with time. Pasquier should let time alone sanction his book!

These startling lines show us the gulf that divides our conception of history from the one that was held by ancient historians and was still current among Pasquier's contemporaries. For them, as for the ancient Greeks, historical truth was a vulgate* authenticated by consensus over the ages. This consensus sanctioned the truth as it sanctioned the reputation of those writers held to be classical or even, I imagine, the tradition of the Church. Far from having to establish the truth by means of references, Pasquier should have waited to be recognized as an authentic text himself. By putting his notes at the bottom of the page, by furnishing proofs as the jurists do, he indiscreetly sought to force the consensus of posterity concerning his work. Given such a conception of historical truth, one cannot claim that the distinction between primary and secondary sources is neglected or even that it is unknown and awaiting discovery. It simply has no meaning or application, and if this supposed lapse had been brought to the attention of these historians, they would have answered that they had no use for it. I do not say that they wouldn't have been wrong; only that, since their conception of the truth was not our own, their omission cannot be used as an explanation.

To understand this conception of history as tradition or vulgate we can compare it to the very similar way in which ancient authors—or even Pascal's *Pensées* of a century and a half ago—were published. What was printed was the received text, the vulgate. Pascal's manuscript was accessible to any publisher, but no one went to the Bibliothèque du Roi to consult it; one simply reprinted the traditional text. The publishers of Latin and Greek texts had to rely on manuscripts, but, for all that, they did not establish the genealogical relationships among the copies. They did not attempt to base the text on completely critical foundations and proceed from a *tabula rasa*. They took a ''good manuscript,'' sent it to the printer, and confined themselves to improving the details of the traditional text by referring

* common, commonly accepted

to other manuscripts they had consulted or discovered. Instead of reestablishing the text, they copied or improved the accepted version. In their accounts of the Peloponnesian War or the legendary first centuries of Roman history, the ancient historians copied one another. This happened not simply because, lacking other sources and authentic documents, they were reduced to such an undertaking; for we, who have access to even fewer documents and are reduced to the statements of these historians, do not necessarily believe them. For us their texts are simply sources, while the ancient historians considered the version transmitted by their predecessors as tradition. Even had they been able to, they would not have sought to rework this tradition but only to improve it. Moreover, for the periods for which they did have documents, they either used them not at all or used them much less than we would and in a completely different way.

Thus, Livy and Dionysius of Halicarnassus imperturbably narrated the four obscure centuries of earliest Roman history by compiling everything their predecessors had stated without ever asking, "Is it true?" They limited themselves to removing details that seemed false or, rather, unlikely or unreal. They presumed that their predecessors were telling the truth. It made no difference that this predecessor wrote several hundred years after the events had taken place. Dionysius and Livy never asked the question that seems so elementary to us: "But how does he know that?" Could they have supposed that this forerunner himself had predecessors, the first of whom *had* been a witness to the actual events? Not at all. They knew very well that the earliest Roman historians had lived four hundred years after Romulus and, furthermore, they did not care. The tradition was there and it was the truth; that was all. If they had learned how this tradition had originally taken form among the first Roman historians—what sources, legends, and memories had been blended in their crucible— they would have seen this as merely the prehistory of the tradition. It would not have made a more authentic text in their eyes. The materials of a tradition are not the tradition itself, which always emerges as a text, a tale carrying authority. History is born as tradition, not built up from source materials. We have seen that, according to Pausanias, the memory of an epoch is ultimately lost if those near the great ones neglect to relate the history of their time, and in the preface to his *War of the Jews* Flavius Josephus says that the most praiseworthy historian is the one who recounts the events of his own day for the benefit of posterity. Why was it more meritorious to write contemporary history than the history of past centuries? The past already has its historians, while the present awaits a historian who will constitute a historical source and establish the tradition. We see that an ancient historian does not use sources and documents; he is source and document himself. Or, rather, history is not built up from sources but consists in reproducing what historians say about it by correcting or possibly completing what they have communicated.

It sometimes happens that an ancient historian notes that his "authorities" diverge on some point or even that he has abandoned his own attempt to know the truth on this point because the versions differ so much. But these displays of critical spirit do not form an apparatus of proofs and variants underlying his text in the modern manner of a scholarly apparatus. They are nothing but hopeless or dubious spots, suspicious details. The ancient historian believes first; his doubts are reserved for details in which he can no longer believe.

It also happens that an ancient historian cites or transcribes a document or describes some archeological object. He does so either to add a detail to the tradition or to illustrate his account and open a parenthesis as a kindness to the reader. Livy does both at once in his book 4. He wonders whether Cornelius Cossus, who killed the Etruscan king of Veii in single combat, was a tribune, as all the authorities said, or whether he was a consul. He opts for the second solution because the inscription on the king's cuirass, consecrated by the victor Cossus in a temple, said "consul": "I have heard," he writes, "that Augustus Caesar, founder and restorer of all our temples, entered the shrine . . . and himself read the inscription on the linen corselet, and I have felt, in consequence, that it would be almost a sacrilege to deprive Cossus of so great a witness to his spoils as Caesar." Livy did not consult any documents. He encountered one by chance, or, rather, he received the emperor's testimony on the subject. This document is less a source of knowledge than an archeological curiosity and relic in which the sovereign's prestige joins with that of a past hero. Often early historians and even those of today cite still visible monuments from the past in this manner, less as proof for their assertions than as illustrations that take on the light and brightness of history more than they actually illuminate it.

Since a historian is an authority for his successors, they may criticize him on occasion. This is not because they have reexamined his whole enterprise, but because they have found errors and are rectifying them. They do not rebuild; they correct. Or they may demolish him. For the finding of errors can be a judgment founded on presumed intentions. In other words, one does not criticize an interpretation of the whole or a detail, but one can undertake to destroy a reputation, to sap an unmerited authority. Does Herodotus' account deserve its authority, or is the author only a liar? As in matters of orthodoxy, so too in questions of authority or tradition: it is all or nothing.

An ancient historian does not cite his authorities, for he feels that he is a potential authority himself. We would like to know where Polybius finds all that he knows. We are even more curious each time his account, or that of Thucydides, takes on a beauteous precision that seems too true to be real because it conforms to some political or strategic reality. When a text is a vulgate, it is tempting to confuse what the author has actually written with what he ought to have written to be worthy of himself. When history is a vulgate, it is difficult to distinguish what actually occurred from what could not have happened according to the truth of things. Each event conforms to type, and this is why the history of the obscure eras of Rome is strewn with extremely elaborate accounts, whose details are to reality what Viollet-le-Duc's restorations are to authenticity. A similar conception of historical reconstitution offered forgers, as we will see, facilities that academic historiography no longer provides.

If we may be permitted to make a supposition about the birthplace of this program of truth in which history is a vulgate, we believe that the ancient historians' respect for the tradition transmitted by their predecessors can be explained by the fact that for them history is born, not out of controversy—as it is with us—but from inquiry (and that is precisely the meaning of the Greek word *historia*). When one inquires (whether as traveler, geographer, ethnographer, or reporter), one can only say, "Here is what I found, here is what I was told by generally reliable sources." It would be futile to include the list of informants. Who would check them? One bases one's estimation of a journalist not on his respect for his sources but on an internal critique or a detail where he has been caught in a blatant error or lapse into partiality. Those strange lines of Estienne Pasquier would not be so surprising had they been applied to a modern reporter, and it would be pleasant to pursue the analogy between ancient history and the deontology or methodology of modern journalism. A reporter adds nothing to his credibility by including his informant's identity. We judge his value on internal criteria. We need only read him to know whether he is intelligent, impartial, or precise and whether he has a broad cultural background. It is exactly in this way that Polybius in book 12 judges and condemns his predecessor Timaeus. He does not discuss the details, except in one case, the foundation of Locris, where, by a happy coincidence, he was able to retrace Timaeus' steps. A good historian, says Thucydides, does not blindly welcome all the traditions he encounters;[16] he must be able to verify his sources, as our reporters say.

However, the historian does not lay out the whole proceeding before his readers. The more demanding he is of himself, the less he will do so. Herodotus likes to report the various contradictory traditions that he gathered. Thucydides almost never does this; he relates only the one he holds to be valid.[17] He takes responsibility for deciding. When he categorically states that the Athenians are mistaken concerning the murder of Pisistratus and gives the version he believes to be true, he restricts himself to stating it.[18] He does not offer any hint of proof. Moreover, it is hard to see how he could have found a means to verify his statements for his readers.

Modern historians propose an interpretation of the facts and give the reader a way to verify the information and formulate a different opinion. The ancient historians take this burden on themselves and do not leave the task to the reader. This is their office. They discriminate very well, whatever one may say, between primary sources (eyewitness accounts or, failing that, tradition) and secondary sources, but they keep these details to themselves. For their readers were not historians, any more than newspaper readers are journalists. Both kinds of readers have confidence in the professional.

When and why did the relation between the historian and his readers change? When and why did references begin to appear? I am not a great expert on modern history, but several details have struck me. Gassendi does not give any references in his *Syntagma philosophiae Epicureae*. He paraphrases or develops Cicero, Hermarchus, and Origen, and the reader cannot tell whether he is being presented with the thoughts of Epicurus himself or those of Gassendi. This is because Gassendi is not being erudite but wants to revive Epicureanism in its eternal truth and, with it, the Epicurean sect. Bossuet, on the other hand, in his *Histoire des variations des églises protestantes,* gives references, and Jurieu gives them, as well, in his response. These, however, are works of controversy. That is the key word. The habit of citing authorities, of scholarly annotation, was not invented by historians but came from theological controversy and juridical practice, where Scripture, the Pandects, or trial proceedings were cited. In the *Summa contra Gentiles,* Aquinas does not refer to passages from Aristotle; he takes responsibility for reinterpreting them and regards them as the very truth, which is anonymous. On the other hand, he cites Scripture, which is Revelation and not the truth of anonymous reason. In his admirable commentary on the *Theodosian Code* in 1695, Godefroy gives his references. This legal historian, as we would call him, considered himself a jurist, not a historian. In short, scholarly annotation has a litigious and polemical origin. Proofs were flaunted about before they were shared with other members of the ''scientific community.'' The main reason for this shift is the rise of the university, with its increasingly exclusive monopoly on intellectual activity. Social and economic causes are at work. Landholders, such as Montaigne or Montesquieu, who were men of leisure, no longer exist. And it is no longer honorable to live as the dependent of a lord instead of working.

Now, at the university the historian no longer writes for the common reader, as journalists or ''writers'' do, but instead writes for other historians, his colleagues. This was not the case for ancient historians. Thus the latter have an apparently lax attitude toward scientific rigor that we find shocking or surprising. In the eighth of the ten books that make up his great work, Pausanias finally writes, ''When I began to write my history, I was inclined to count these legends as foolishness; but on getting as far as Arcadia I grew to hold a more thoughtful view of them, which is this: in the days of old, those Greeks who were considered wise spoke their sayings not straight out but in riddles, and so the legends about Cronos I conjectured to be one sort of Greek wisdom.'' This tardy confession shows in retrospect that Pausanias did not believe a word of the innumerable unlikely legends that he had calmly put forth in the preceding six hundred pages. We think of another avowal, no less tardy, coming from Herodotus at the end of the seventh of his nine books. Did the Argives betray the Greek cause in 480 B.C., and did they ally themselves with the Persians, who claimed to have the same mythic ancestor as they, i.e., Perseus? "My business," writes Herodotus, "is to record what people say; but I am by no means bound to believe it—and that may be taken to apply to this book as a whole."[19]

If a modern historian presented to the scientific community facts or legends he himself did not believe, the integrity of science would be weakened. The ancient historians have, if not a different idea of integrity, at least different readers, who are not professionals and who form a public that is as heterogeneous as the readership of a newspaper. Thus they have a right, even a duty, to their reserve, and they have some room in which to maneuver. They do not express the truth itself; it is up to their readers to form their own idea. This is one of the numerous, barely visible particularities that reveal that, despite great similarities, the historical genre in Antiquity is very different from what it is today. The audience of the ancient historians is varied. Some readers seek entertainment; others read history with a more critical eye; some are even professionals in politics or strategy. Each historian makes a choice: to write for everyone, by tactfully dealing with different categories of readers, or to specialize, as Thucydides and Polybius did, in technically safe information that will always produce data useful to politicians and military men. But the choice had been given. Moreover, the heterogeneity of the public gave the historian some leeway. He could present the truth in harsh or soft colors as he liked, without, however, betraying it. Therefore one must not be surprised or shocked at the letter, amply discussed by modern commentators, in which Cicero asks Lucceius "to elevate the actions of his consulate" more, perhaps, than he would have done and not "to take too much account of the law of the historical genre." A simple matter among friends, which does not exceed what one could, without too much dishonesty, ask of a journalist, who will always have part of his audience on his side.

Behind the apparent question of scientific method or integrity lies another: the relation of the historian to his readers. Momigliano speculates that a new attitude toward documents appeared during the Late Empire and that it heralded the future method of scientifically directed history; the *Augustan History* and especially Eusebius' *Ecclesiastical History* display evidence of a "new value attached to documents."[20] I confess that these works have left me with a rather different impression. The *Augustan History* does not cite its sources; from time to time it transcribes a text from a famous author as a curiosity and monument of Antiquity. The Alexandrians had already done this. Moreover, what Eusebius transcribes are not truly sources but excerpts. He compiles "partial accounts," as he himself calls them in the first lines of his history. It is a setting of precious pieces in which the author avoids the trouble of writing the history by copying his forerunners. Far from evincing a new attitude, Eusebius confirms the "absolute objectivity," in Renan's phrase, with which late Antiquity regarded the historical work.[21] We can already see the method of compiling massive excerpts in Porphyry (who preserved texts by Theophrastus and Hermarchus in this manner), and Eusebius also resorts to it in his *Evangelical Preparation* (which makes it possible for us to read Oenomaus the Cynic and Diogenianus the Peripatetic).

The aim for objectivity delimited the historian's role: before the age of controversy, before the time of Nietzsche and Max Weber, facts existed. The historian had neither to interpret (since facts existed) nor prove (because facts are not the stakes of a controversy). He had only to report the facts, either as a "reporter" or a compiler. For that he did not require vertiginous intellectual gifts. He needed only three virtues, which any good journalist possesses: diligence, competence, and impartiality. He must diligently inquire into books, question witnesses, if any still could be found, or gather traditions or "myths." His competence on political matters, such as strategy or geography, permits him to understand the actions of public figures and to criticize his information. His impartiality will prevent him from lying, either by commission or omission. His work and his virtues mean that the historian, unlike the crowd, will know the truth concerning the past. For, as Pausanias says, "There are many false beliefs current among the mass of mankind, since they are ignorant of historical science and consider trustworthy whatever they have heard from childhood in choruses and tragedies; one of these is about Theseus, who in fact himself became king, and afterwards, when Menestheus was dead, the descendants of Theseus remained rulers even to the fourth generation."[22]

As we see, Pausanias separated the grain from the chaff. He extracted the authentic kernel from the legend of Theseus. How did he

* rotary, revolving ⇒ inconstant, unstable

do this? By means of what we would call the doctrine of present things. The past resembles the present, or, in other words, the marvelous does not exist. Now today, men with bulls' heads are rarely seen, and kings do exist; therefore the Minotaur never existed, and Theseus was simply a king. For Pausanias does not doubt Theseus' historicity, and Aristotle, five hundred years before him, did not doubt it either.[23] Before taking the critical attitude that reduces myth to verisimilitude, the average Greek had a different viewpoint. According to his mood, mythology was either a collection of old wives' tales, or else the supernatural provoked a stance in which questions of historicity or fiction had no meaning.

The critical attitude toward myth, that of Pausanias, Aristotle, and even Herodotus, consists of seeing in myth an oral tradition or a historical source that must be criticized.[24] The method is an excellent one, but it raised a false problem that dogged the Ancients for a millennium. It took a historical mutation, Christianity, to enable them not to resolve the issue but to forget it. This problem was the following: mythical tradition transmits an authentic kernel that over the ages has been overgrown with legends. These legends, not the kernel itself, are the source of the difficulty. As we have seen, it is with respect to these legendary additions, and only them, that the thought of Pausanias evolved.[25]

Thus, the question of the criticism of mythical traditions is poorly formulated. A writer such as Pausanias only seems to resemble Fontenelle, who, far from sorting out the wheat from the chaff, speculated that everything in the legends was false.[26] And the resemblance between ancient criticism of myth and our own is equally deceptive. In legend we see history magnified by the ''spirit of the people.'' We view a particular myth as the epic aggrandizement of a great event, such as the ''Dorian invasion.'' But for a Greek the same myth is a truth that has been altered by popular naïveté. At its authentic core are small true details, such as the names of heroes and their genealogies, which contain nothing of the marvelous.

The paradox is all too familiar. If legends are thought to transmit collective memories, the historicity of the Trojan War is believable. If these legends are considered as fiction, the historicity of that war is unacceptable, and the equivocal finds of the archeologists will be otherwise interpreted. Underlying the issues of method and positivity we find a more fundamental question: What is myth? Is it altered history? History that has been amplified? A collective mythomania? Is it allegory? What was myth to the Greeks?[27] This is the moment for us to note not only that the feeling of truth is a capacious one (which easily comprehends myth) but also that "truth" means many things . . . and can even encompass fictional literature.

2
The Plurality and Analogy of True Worlds

For Greek mythology, whose connections with religion were very loose,[28] was basically nothing but a very popular literary genre, a vast realm of literature, mainly oral in character—if, indeed, the term "literature" can be applied when the distinction between fiction and reality had yet to be made and the legendary element was serenely accepted.

Reading Pausanias, one understands what mythology was: the most insignificant little village described by our author has its legend concerning some local curiosity, natural or cultural.[29] This legend, invented by an unknown storyteller, was later discovered by one of those innumerable local scholars whom Pausanias read (he called them "exegetes"). Each of these authors or storytellers knew the work of his colleagues, since the various legends have the same heroes and take up the same themes, and the divine or heroic genealogies are largely in agreement or at least do not suffer from blatant contradictions. This unknown literature recalls another one: the lives of the local saints and martyrs from the Merovingian era up to the *Golden Legend*. Arnold van Gennep has shown that these apocryphal hagiographies, which the Bollandists had so much trouble refuting, were in reality works of an extremely popular character. They abound with abducted princesses (horribly tortured or saved by saintly knights), along with snobbery, sex, sadism, and adventure. The people adored these accounts. Artists illustrated them, and an extensive literature in verse and prose took them up.[30]

These legendary worlds were accepted as true in the sense that they were not doubted, but they were not accepted the way that everyday reality is. For the faithful, the lives of the martyrs were filled with marvels situated in an ageless past, defined only in that it was earlier, outside of, and different from the present. It was the "time of the pagans.'' The same was true of the Greek myths. They took place "earlier,'' during the heroic generations, when the gods still took part in human affairs. Mythological space and time were secretly different from our own.[31] A Greek put the gods "in heaven,'' but he would have been astounded to see them in the sky. He would have been no less astounded if someone, using time in its literal sense, told him that Hephaestus had just remarried or that Athena had aged a great deal lately. Then he would have realized that in his own eyes mythic time had only a vague analogy with daily temporality; he would also have thought that a kind of lethargy had always kept him from recognizing this difference. The analogy between these temporal worlds disguises their hidden plurality. It is not self-evident that humanity has a past, known or unknown. One does not perceive the limit of the centuries, held in memory, any more than one perceives the line bounding the visual field. One does not see the obscure centuries stretching beyond this horizon. One simply stops seeing, and that is all. The heroic generations are found on the other side of this temporal horizon in another world. This is the mythical world in whose existence thinkers from Thucydides or Hecataeus to Pausanias or Saint Augustine will continue to believe—except that they will stop seeing it as another world and will want to reduce it to the mode of the present.[32] They will act as if myth pertained to the same realm of belief as history.[33]

On the other hand, those who were not thinkers saw beyond the horizon of collective memory a world that was even more beautiful than that of the good old days, too beautiful to be real. This mythical world was not empirical; it was noble. This is not to say that it incarnated or symbolized "values.'' The heroic generations did not cultivate virtue any more than do the men of today, but they had more "value'' than the men of today. A hero is more real than a man, just as, in Proust's eyes, a duchess has more value than a *bourgeoise*.

Pindar offers a good example of such snobbery (if we may resort to humor for brevity's sake). The problem is well known. What is the source of the unity, if indeed there is any, in Pindar's *epinikia?* Why does the poet choose to present to the victor a myth whose relation to the subject is no longer apparent? Is this the poet's royal whim? Or is the athlete only a pretext that allows Pindar to express views that are dear to him? Or, again, is the myth an allegory, and does it allude to some particularity of the victor or his ancestors? H. Fränkel offers the valid explanation: Pindar elevates the victor and his victory to a higher

* victory songs, triumphal odes

world, that of the poet.[34] For, as a poet, Pindar is the familiar of the world of gods and heroes. He raises the victor, this worthy plebeian, up to his world by treating him as an equal and by speaking to him of this mythical world, which henceforth will be his, thanks to Pindar, who has introduced him to it. There is not necessarily any close relationship between the victor's personality and the matters on which the poet speaks to him. Pindar does not make a point of ensuring that the myth always contains a delicate allusion to the victor's person. What is important is that he treats the victor as a peer by speaking familiarly to him of this mythical world.

In our century the natural tendency is to explain the products of the mind in sociological terms. When examining a work we ask, ''What was it meant to bring to society?'' This is acting too quickly. We must not reduce the explanation of literature, or its hermeneutics, to a sociology of literature. In *Paideia,* Werner Jaeger seems to have telescoped his case. According to him, when the Hellenic aristocracy was engaged in its last battles, it found in Pindar a poet it could claim as its own, one who could satisfy a social need. In fact, according to Jaeger, this aristocratic class of warriors saw itself elevated with its values to the world of myth. The heroes would thus have been models for these warriors. Pindar would have praised mythical heroes to exalt the hearts of his noble listeners. In his verse the mythical world would be the sublime image of this aristocracy.

Is this true? We easily note that Pindar uses myth not at all to exalt the aristocracy but to raise his own position vis-à-vis his listeners. As a poet he deigns to elevate to his own level the victor whom he celebrates. It is not the victor who performs this feat. In Pindar the myth does not fulfill a social function and does not contain a message. It plays what semiotics has only recently called a pragmatic role: it establishes a certain relationship between the listeners and the poet himself. Literature is not reducible to a relationship of cause and effect with society any more than language is reducible to a code or to information, for it, too, serves as an illocution, i.e., the establishment of different specific relationships with the listener. To promise or command are attitudes that cannot be reduced to the content of the message; they do not consist in giving information about a promise or a command. Literature does not reside entirely in its content. When Pindar sings the praises of the heroes, he does not give his listeners a message relating to their values and to themselves; he establishes a certain relationship with them in which he, a poet to whom myths are open, occupies the dominant position. Pindar speaks from the top, and it is just for that reason that he can bestow praise, honor a victor, and raise him to his own height. Myth brings about an illocution of praise.

Far from assimilating the aristocracy to heroic mythical figures, Pindar vigorously separates the mythical world from that of mortal men. He never ceases to remind his noble listeners that men are worth much less than the gods and that modesty is vital. One cannot equal the gods without hubris. Let us look at the *Tenth Pythian*. Does Pindar offer Perseus as a model to the warrior he is celebrating? No. He speaks of remarkable legends, of a faraway and inaccessible people, of the superhuman exploits of Perseus, who was aided by a goddess. More than by their merits, the heroes judged worthy of divine support are honored by the gods' favor, which must encourage modesty in mortals; for even the heroes were unable to succeed without the aid of some divinity. Pindar magnifies his victor's glory by exalting this other, higher world, where glory itself is greater. Is this superior world a model or a lesson in modesty? One or the other, according to the use a preacher would make of it, and Pindar, who is not a preacher, makes it into a pedestal. He elevates both the victor and the celebration by elevating himself. It is precisely because the mythical world is definitively other, inaccessible, different, and remarkable that the problem of its authenticity is suspended, and Pindar's listeners float between wonderment and credulity. This is no fairyland; for if Perseus were given as a model in the manner of Bayard, this different world would immediately be condemned as pure fiction, and only the Don Quixotes would still believe in it.

There is a problem, then, that we cannot avoid: Did the Greeks believe in these tales? More specifically, did they distinguish between what they held as authentic—the historicity of the Trojan War or the existence of Agamemnon and Zeus—and the obvious inventions of the poet, who desired to please his audience? Did they listen with the same ear to the geographical lists and catalogues of ships and to the tale, worthy of Boccaccio, of the amorous adventures of Aphrodite and Ares caught in bed by her husband? If they really believed in myth, did they at least know how to distinguish fable from fiction? But, precisely, it would be necessary to know whether literature or religion are more fictitious than history or physics, and vice versa. Let us say that a work of art is accepted as true in its way, even when it passes for fiction. For truth is a homonym that should be used only in the plural. There are only different programs of truth, and Fustel de Coulanges is neither more nor less true than Homer, even if differently so. Only, it is of truth as it is with Being, according to Aristotle: it is homonymical and analogical, for all truths seem analogous among themselves, so that Racine seems to us to have portrayed the truth of the human heart.

Let us take as our starting point the fact that all legends—the Trojan War, the *Thebaïd,* or the expedition of the Argonauts—passed for being completely authentic. Thus a listener to the *Iliad* was in the position of the modern reader of a historical novel. The latter is recognizable by the fact that its authors utilize authentic events; if they write of the love between Napoleon Bonaparte and the Empress Josephine, they couch it in dialogue and put words in the mouths of the Corsican and his beloved that have no literal truth. The reader knows this, makes light of it, or does not even think about it. This does not lead him to view the story as fiction. Napoleon existed and truly loved Josephine. The overall credit is sufficient, and he does not want to carp at details that, as they say in New Testament exegesis, are merely "editorial." Homer's listeners believed in the overall truthfulness of the account and did not disdain the pleasure of the tale of Ares and Aphrodite.

The fact remains that Napoleon's biography is not only true but probable. On the other hand, one would say that the world of the *Iliad,* whose temporality is that of tales and where gods enter into human affairs, is a fictional universe. Indeed; but Madame Bovary truly believed that Naples was a different world from our own. There happiness flourished twenty-four hours a day with the density of a Sartrean *en-soi.* Others have believed that in Maoist China men and things do not have the same humble, quotidian reality that they have here at home; unfortunately, they take this fairy-tale truth for a program of political truth. A world cannot be inherently fictional; it can be fictional only according to whether one believes in it or not. The difference between fiction and reality is not objective and does not pertain to the thing itself; it resides in us, according to whether or not we subjectively see in it a fiction. The object is never unbelievable in itself, and its distance from "the" reality cannot shock us; for, as truths are always analogical, we do not even see it.

According to a certain program of truth, that of deductive and quantified physics, Einstein is true in our eyes. But if we believe in the *Iliad,* it is no less true according to its own mythical program. The same can be said for *Alice in Wonderland.* For, even if we consider *Alice* and the plays of Racine as fiction, while we are reading them we believe; we weep at the theater. The world of *Alice* and its fairy-tale program is offered to us as a realm as plausible and true as our own— as real in relation to itself, so to speak. We have shifted the sphere of truth, but we are still within the true or its analogy. This is why realism in literature is at once a fake (it is not reality), a useless exertion (the fairy world would seem no less real), and the most extreme sophistication (to fabricate the real with our real: how baroque!). Far from being opposed to the truth, fiction is only its by-product. All we need to do is open the *Iliad* and we enter into the story, as they say, and lose our bearings. The only subtlety is that later on we do not believe. There are societies where, once the book is closed, the reader goes on believing; there are others where he does not.

We change truths when we shift from our everyday life into the domain of Racine, but we do not perceive this. We have just written a jealous, interminable, and confused letter, which we suddenly retract an hour later by telegram, and we have been transported into the realm of Racine or Catullus, where a cry of jealousy, as dense as Sartre's *en-soi,* sounds without a false note for four lines. How true this cry is to us! Literature is a magic carpet that takes us from one truth to another, but we travel in a state of lethargy. When, having arrived at a new truth, we awaken, we still believe we are in the old realm. This is why it is impossible to make the naïve reader understand that Racine and Catullus—and Propertius even less—have neither depicted the human heart nor told their own life-story. Yet in their own way these readers are right; all truths boil down to one. *Madame Bovary* is "a masterpiece for anyone who has heard confession in the provinces." It is the analogy among systems of truth that permits us to enter into novelistic fictions, to find their heroes "alive," and to take interest in the thought and philosophies of other times. And in those of today. These truths, that of the *Iliad* and that of Einstein, are born of the imagination and are not the product of some natural illumination.

Literature before there was literature, neither true nor fictitious because it is external to but nobler than the real world, myth displays another characteristic: as its name indicates, it is an anonymous tale that can be collected and repeated but that can have no author. This is what rational minds, beginning with Thucydides, will interpret as historical "tradition," as a memory that contemporaries of the events have transmitted to their descendants. Before being thus disguised as history, myth was something else. It consisted, not in communicating what one had seen, but in repeating what "was said" of the gods and heroes. How can myth be formally recognized? By the fact that the exegete speaks of this superior world by putting his own words into indirect discourse: "People say that . . . ," "The Muse sings that . . . ," "*Logos* tells us that . . . ." The speaker does not appear directly, for the Muse herself only "retells" or reminds the writer of this tale, which is its own progenitor.[35] When it comes to gods and heroes, the only source of knowledge is the "they say," and this source has a mysterious authority. Not that impostors cannot be found: the Muses, O Hesiod, know how to speak the truth and how to lie.[36] Poets who lie still refer to the Muses, who inspired Homer as well as Hesiod.

Myth is information. There are informed people who have alighted, not on a revelation, but simply on some vague information they have chanced upon. If they are poets, it will be the Muses, their appointed informants, who will tell them what is known and said. For all that, myth is not a revelation from above, nor is it arcane knowledge. The Muse only repeats to them what is known—which, like a natural resource, is available to all who seek it.

Myth is not a specific mode of thought. It is nothing more than knowledge obtained through information, which is applied to realms that for us would pertain to argument or experiment. As Oswald Ducrot writes in *Dire et ne pas dire,* information is an illocution that can be completed only if the receiver recognizes the speaker's competence and honesty beforehand, so that, from the very outset, a piece of information is situated beyond the alternative between truth and falsehood. To see this mode of knowledge function, we need only read the admirable Father Huc's account of how he converted the Tibetans a century and a half ago:

> We had adopted a completely historical mode of instruction, taking care to exclude anything that suggested argument and the spirit of contention; proper names and very precise dates

made much more of an impression on them than the most logical reasoning. When they knew the names Jesus, Jerusalem, and Pontius Pilate and the date 4000 years after Creation, they no longer doubted the mystery of the Redemption and the preaching of the Gospel. Furthermore, we never noticed that mysteries or miracles gave them the slightest difficulty. We are convinced that it is through teaching and not the method of argument that one can work efficaciously toward the conversion of the Infidel.

Similarly, in Greece there existed a domain, the supernatural, where everything was to be learned from people who knew. It was composed of events, not abstract truths against which the listener could oppose his own reason. The facts were specific: heroes' names and patronyms were always indicated, and the location of the action was equally precise (Pelion, Cithaeron, Titaresius . . . place names have a music in Greek mythology). This state of affairs may have lasted more than a thousand years. It did not change because the Greeks discovered reason or invented democracy but because the map of the field of knowledge was turned upside down by the creation of new powers of affirmation (historical investigation and speculative physics) that competed with myth and, unlike it, expressly offered the alternative between true and false.

Such is the mythology that each ancient historian criticizes without discarding his taste for the marvelous—far from it—but without recognizing its character, either. He takes it for historiography. Regarding *mythos* as a simple local "tradition," he treats mythical temporality as if it were historical time. This is not all. The historian also deals with another type of mythological literature, which appeared in epic verse or prose. These are the mythical genealogies, beginning with Hesiod's *Great Eoiae,* and etiologies, stories of the foundation of cities, and local histories and epics. This literature flourished from the sixth century onward and survived in Asia Minor under the Antonines and beyond.[37] Produced by men of letters, it catered less to the taste for the marvelous than to the search for origins. Think of our own legend of the Trojan origins of the Frankish monarchy, from Frédégaire up to Ronsard. Since it was the Trojans who founded kingdoms worthy of the name, they must also have founded the Frankish monarchy. And since the onomasticon of place

vocabulary or collection of names or nouns formerly including a lexicon or dictionary but now applied to a vocabulary or systematic list of proper nouns, esp. persons

names originates in men's names, the Trojan in question must have been named Francion.

Pausanias used an epic poet of the high Hellenistic era, Rhianus, and the historian Myron of Priene in the same manner for his research on Messenia.[38] For Arcadia he followed a "genealogy told by the Arcadians," i.e., a tradition supposedly recorded by Asius, a poet of the Epic Cycle.[39] Our author thus learned of the dynasty of the Arcadian kings for many generations, from Pelasgus, a contemporary of Cecrops, up to the time of the Trojan War. He knows their names, their patronyms, and their children's names. He sets this genealogy against the unfolding of historical time and is then able to establish that Oenotria, founded by Oenotrus, Lycaon's son of the third generation, is necessarily by far the oldest colony founded by the Greeks.

This genealogical literature, in which Pausanias found a historiography, in reality tells of *aitiai,* origins, the establishment of the order of the world. The implicit idea (still found in book 5 of Lucretius) is that our world is finished, formed and complete (as my child said to me with some amazement, while watching masons at work, "Papa, so all the houses haven't been built yet?").[40] By definition, this establishment occurred before the dawn of history, in the mythical time of the hero. Everything focuses on telling how a man, a custom, or a city came into being. Once born, a city has only to live its historic life, which is no longer a concern of etiology.*

Etiology, which a Polybius[41] would find childish, was thus limited to explaining a thing by its beginning: a city, by its founder; a rite, by an incident that formed a precedent, for it has been repeated; a people, by a first individual born from the earth or a first king. Between this first fact and our historical era, which begins with the Trojan War, stretches the succession of mythical generations. The mythographer reconstitutes—or rather invents—a seamless royal genealogy that spans the whole mythical age. When he has invented it, he feels the satisfaction that comes from complete knowledge. Where does he get the proper names that he affixes to every branch of his genealogical tree? From his imagination, sometimes from allegory, and, more often, from place names. The rivers, mountains, and cities of a country come from the names of the original people who lived there, who were thought to have been the kings of the country rather than its sole inhabitants. The ageless human trail found in toponyms originates in the human onomasticon of mythical times. When the

* or aetiology - investigation of causes or reasons

name of a river is derived from a man's name, we are brought back to the original human presence dating from the time when the region became a human territory.[42]

But what caused the name of a king of old to pass to, or be given to, this river? This is precisely what the genealogist would never ask. Verbal analogy is sufficient, and his preferred mode of explanation is archetypal. One might as well wonder what concrete relationship exists between Faunus and the Fauns, between Hellen and the Hellenes, between Pelasgus and the Pelasgians, or, in the following etiological pastiche, between Elephant and the elephants: "In the beginning the elephants had no trunk, but a god pulled on Elephant's nose to punish him for some trickery, and since that day all elephants have a trunk." Pausanias no longer understands this archetypal logic, and he takes the archetype, who, like Adam, was the only being, for the first king of the country. "The Arcadians," he says,

> say that Pelasgus was the first inhabitant of this land. It is natural to suppose that others accompanied Pelasgus and that he was not by himself; for otherwise he would have been a king without any subjects to rule over. However, in stature and in prowess, in bearing and in wisdom, Pelasgus excelled his fellows, and for this reason, I think, he was chosen to be king by them. Asius the poet says of him: *The godlike Pelasgus on the wooded mountains / Black earth gave up, that the race of mortals / might exist.*[43]

These few lines offer us a kind of "collage": old mythical truth is plastered over the type of rationalism practiced by Pausanias, who seems largely unaware of the difference between these materials.

3

The Social Distribution of Knowledge and the Modalities of Belief

How could people believe in all these legends, and did they truly believe in them? This is not a subjective question; modalities of belief are related to the ways in which truth is possessed. Throughout the ages a plurality of programs of truth has existed, and it is these programs, involving different distributions of knowledge, that explain the subjective degrees of intensity of beliefs, the bad faith, and the contradictions that coexist in the same individual.[44] We agree with Michel Foucault on this point. The history of ideas truly begins with the historicization of the philosophical idea of truth.

There is no such thing as a sense of the real. Furthermore, there is no reason—quite the contrary—for representing what is past or foreign as analogous to what is current or near. The content of myth was situated in a noble and platonic temporality, as foreign to individual experience and individual interests as are government proclamations or esoteric theories learned at school and accepted at face value. In other respects, myth was information obtained from someone else. This was the primary attitude of the Greeks toward myth; in this modality of belief they were depending on someone else's word. Two effects can be noted. First, there is a sort of lethargic indifference, or at least hesitation, about truth and fiction. And this dependence ends up leading to rebellion: people wish to judge things for themselves, according to their own experience. It is precisely this principle of current things that will cause the Greeks to measure the marvelous against everyday reality and pass on to other modalities of belief.

Can belief divorced from action be sincere? When we are separated from something by an abyss, we ourselves do not know whether we believe in it or not. Pindar was already hesitating about myth, and the language of the *Tenth Pythian*, respectful as it is, betrays some wavering: "Neither by land nor sea do we find the route that leads to the celebrations of the peoples of the Great North. The daring Perseus, in old times, could easily go to them, to the fortunate ones. Athena was his guide, and he killed the Gorgon! On my part, nothing surprises me or seems unbelievable when the gods bring it to pass."

The most widespread modality of belief occurs when one trusts the word of another. I believe that Tokyo exists, although I have not yet been there, because I cannot see how the geographers and travel agencies would gain anything by tricking me.[45] This modality can endure as long as the believer trusts the professionals or until there are no professionals to make laws on the subject. Westerners, at least those among us who are not bacteriologists, believe in germs and increase the sanitary precautions we take for the same reason that the Azande believe in witches and multiply their magical precautions against them: their belief is based on trust. For Pindar's or Homer's contemporaries, truth was defined either as it related to daily experience or in terms of the speaker's character: whether it was loyal or treacherous. Statements foreign to experience were neither true nor false. Nor were they falsehoods, for a lie does not exist when the liar gains nothing from it and does us no harm. A disinterested lie is no deception. Myth was a *tertium quid,* neither true nor false. Einstein would be the same for us if his truth did not come from a third source, the realm of professional authority.

In those far-off times this authority had not been born, and theology, physics, and history did not exist. The intellectual universe was exclusively literary. True myths followed the poets' inventions in the minds of the listeners, who listened docilely to the man who knew; they had no interest in separating truth from falsehood and were not shaken by fictions that contradicted no known science. Thus, they listened to true myths and inventions in the same frame of mind. In order to shake his contemporaries out of this lethargy, Hesiod will be obliged to create a stir and proclaim that poets lie; for he wishes, for his own benefit, to constitute a realm of truth, where one will no longer say just anything about the gods.

Given its dissymmetry, belief in someone else's word could in fact support individual enterprises that opposed their truth to the general error or ignorance. This is the case with Hesiod's speculative theogony, which is not a revelation given by the gods. Hesiod received this knowledge from the Muses—that is, from his own reflections. By pondering all that had been said about the gods and the world, he understood many things and was able to establish a true and complete list of genealogies. First were Chaos and Earth, as well as Love; Chaos begat Night, Earth gave birth to Heaven and Oceanus. The latter had forty daughters, whose names Hesiod gives us: Peitho, Admete, Ianthe, the fair Polydora, etc. Many of these genealogies are allegories, and one has the impression that Hesiod takes his god-concepts more seriously than he takes the Olympians. But how does he know so many names and so many details? How does it come to pass that all these old cosmogonies are veritable novels? Because of the dissymmetry that characterizes knowledge based on faith in another. Hesiod knows that we will take him at his word, and he treats himself as he will be treated: he is the first to believe everything that enters his head.

In the matter of great problems, says the *Phaedo,* when one has not been able to find the truth oneself or has not received the revelation of it from some god, one can only adopt the best that has been said or find out from someone who knows.[46] The "people say" of myth thus takes on a different meaning. Myth is no longer knowledge hovering in the air, a natural resource whose captors are distinguished by greater luck or skill. It is a privilege of the great minds, whose teachings are repeated. "It is said that, when one dies, one becomes like the stars in the sky," declares one of Aristophanes' heroes, who has heard tell of the lofty knowledge held by certain sects of the day.[47]

Along with these more or less esoteric speculations, truth based on belief had another type of hero: the solver of riddles. Here we find the first developments of physics or metaphysics—that is, nothing less than the presumed beginnings of Western thought. Developing a physics consisted in finding the key to the riddle of the world;[48] for there was a riddle, and, once it was solved, all secrets would be penetrated at once—or, rather, the mystery would disappear, the scales would fall from our eyes.

For example, here is how Greek tradition depicted the beginnings of philosophy. Thales was the first to find the key to all things: "Everything is water." Was he teaching the unity of the world? Was he on the track that would lead to monism, to the problems of Being and the unity of nature? In fact, if we believe tradition, his thesis was neither metaphysical nor ~~ontological~~ but, instead, allegorical and . . . chemical. Things are made of water in the same way that, for

K ontology: science of being or reality; the branch of knowledge that investigates the nature, essential properties and relations of being, as such.

us, sea salt is made of sodium and chloride. And, since everything is water, everything passes, flows, changes; everything runs away. A strange chemistry: on what can it base a claim to recombine the diversity of its parts in one simple body? It makes no such claim. It is not an explanation but a key, and a key must be simple. Monism? Not even that. It is not monism that leads us to speak of the "key" to an enigma in the singular. Now, a key is not an explanation. While an explanation accounts for a phenomenon, a key makes us forget the riddle. It erases and replaces it in the same way that a clear sentence eclipses an earlier, more confused, and obscure formulation. As Greek philosophical tradition presents him, Thales does not account for the world in its diversity. He gives us its true meaning, "water," and this answer replaces the enigmatic confusion, which is immediately forgotten. For one forgets the text of a riddle; the solution is the whole point.

An explanation is something that is sought and proved. The key of a riddle is guessed and, once guessed, it operates instantaneously. There is not even the possiblity of an argument. The veil falls away, and our eyes are opened. It is only necessary to say "Open sesame." Each of the first physicists of early Greece had opened everything by himself, in a single act. Two hundred years later, Epicurean physics would present a similar case. We can get a glimpse of it in the work of Freud. It is amazing that the strangeness of his work startles us so little: these tracts, unfurling the map of the depths of the psyche, without a shred of proof or argument; without examples, even for purposes of clarification; without the slightest clinical illustration; without any means of seeing where Freud found all that or how he knows it. From observing his patients? Or, more likely, from observing himself? It is not surprising that this archaic work has been carried on in a form of knowledge that is no less archaic: commentary. What else can be done but comment when the key to the enigma has been found? Moreover, only a genius, an inspired man, almost a god, could find the key to such an enigma. Epicurus is a god—yes, a god—proclaims his disciple, Lucretius. The man with the key is believed at his word and will not ask more of himself than his admirers do. His disciples do not continue his work; they transmit it and add nothing. They restrict themselves to defending, illustrating, and applying it.

We have just spoken of masters and disciples. To return from them to the matter of myth itself: incredulity arises from at least two sources, an upsurge of intractability in response to the word of another and the formation of professional centers of truth.

As will still be the case in the eighteenth century, the Greek aristocracy wavered between two attitudes toward legend: to be pragmatic and participate in the popular credulity, for the people believe as docilely as they obey; or else to refuse, on their own account, a humiliating submission, which was perceived as a result of naïveté. Understanding is the first of privileges.

In the first case, the aristocrats also gained the power to appeal to the authority of mythical genealogies: Plato's Lysis had an ancestor who was fathered by Zeus and had received in his house his half-brother, Heracles, another of the god's bastard children.[49] But other fashionable people had the good taste to be enlightened and to think differently from the crowd. Xenophanes does not wish his guests at banquets to fall to quarreling or to spout foolishness, and, as a consequence, he forbids them to speak "of Titans, Giants, Centaurs, of all inventions of the Ancients."[50] The lesson was heard; at the end of Aristophanes' *The Wasps,* a son who tries to inculcate a little social distinction in his father, whose ideas are lower class, tells him that it is not polite to talk about myths at the table. One must speak of human things.[51] Such, he concludes, is the conversation of proper people. Not to believe everything was a Greek quality par excellence: "For centuries past," says Herodotus, "the Greeks have distinguished themselves from less civilized peoples by their greater awareness and lack of foolish credulity."

Unwillingness to accept the word of another is less a matter of class interest than a character trait, and it would be a mistake to see this rebelliousness as an aristocratic privilege. One would be equally mistaken to suppose that it belongs to certain periods that alternate with periods of faith. One need only think of the pages of *Etudes de sociologie religieuse,* in which Gabriel Le Bras analyzes the reports made by bishops of the Old Regime after their diocesan inspections.[52] Each village had its miscreants, who, not daring to fail in their Sunday obligations, remained in the back of the church during the Mass or even stayed outside on the portico. Each society had its doubters, who were more or less numerous and bold, depending on the indulgence displayed by the authorities. Greece had its share, as is attested by a remarkable line from Aristophanes' *The Knights.*[53] A slave despairing over his fate says to his companion in misfortune, "The only thing left to do is to throw ourselves at the feet of the gods,'' and his comrade answers him, ''Indeed! Say, then, do you really believe that there are gods?'' I am not sure that this slave's eyes were opened by the Sophist enlightenment. He belongs to the irreducible fringe of unbelievers who make their refusal less because of reason and the movement of ideas than in reaction to a subtle form of authority, the very same authority that Polybius attributed to the Roman Senate and that is practiced by all those who ally their throne to the altar.[54] Not that religion necessarily has a conservative influence, but some modalities of belief are a form of symbolic obedience. To believe is to obey. The political role of religion is not at all a matter of ideological content.

A second reason for no longer believing everything that was said was that myth, as it pertained to information, was in competition with the specialists in truth, the ''investigators'' or historians who, as professionals, began to carry authority. Now, in their eyes it was necessary for myths to fit with the rest of reality, since they claimed to be real. Herodotus, collecting information in Egypt, discovers a cult of Heracles (for a god is a god everywhere, just as an oak is an oak everywhere; but each people gives it a different name, so that divine names are translated from one language to another, just like common nouns).[55] As the date that the Egyptians assigned to this Heracles did not at all coincide with the legendary chronology of the Greeks, Herodotus tried to resolve the difficulty by inquiring about the date that the Phoenicians attributed to their own Heracles, and his difficulty only grew. All that he was able to conclude was that all men were in agreement about seeing Heracles as a very ancient god and also that one could extricate oneself from the difficulty by distinguishing two of them.

That is not all. ''The Greeks say many other things without thinking. No less credible is a myth that they tell about Heracles; when the latter went to Egypt,'' the inhabitants of this country had apparently attempted to sacrifice him to Zeus, but Heracles would not let them take him and killed them all. Impossible, protests Herodotus. The Egyptians do not make living sacrifices, as anyone who knows their laws is aware. And since Heracles was still only a man, according to what people say (indeed, he became a god only at his death), ''would it be natural for a single man to be able to kill myriads of other men?'' We see just how far Herodotus is from accepting knowledge based on the word of another. Such a source provides information: What is the capital city of this kingdom? What are So-and-So's kinship lines? What are Heracles' dates? Those who inform you are themselves informed, and in this area the important opposition is not between truth and error but between information and ignorance. Except that, in matters of information, a professional investigator does not have the docility of other men. He cross-checks and verifies it. The social distribution of knowledge is thereby transformed; henceforth other men, not wishing to appear untutored, will prefer to consult this professional. And, as the investigator cross-checks information, he imposes the need for coherence on reality. Mythical time can no longer remain secretly different from our own temporality. It is nothing more than the past.

The criticism of myth arises from the methods of inquiry. It has nothing to do either with the Sophistic movement, which ended rather in a criticism of religion and society, or with the cosmologies of physics.

How can such a transformation be explained? I don't know and am not very eager to learn. History has long been defined as an explanatory account, a narrative featuring causes. To explain used to pass for being the sublime part of the historian's craft. Indeed, it was considered that explanation consisted in finding a reason, garbed as a cause—that is, a scheme (the rise of the bourgeoisie, the forces of production, the revolt of the masses) that brought great and exciting ideas into play. But let us suppose that explanation is reduced to envisaging a polygon of minor causes that do not remain constant from one set of circumstances to the next and that do not fill the specific places that a pattern would assign to them in advance. In this case, explanation, which has become circumstantial and anecdotal, would be no more than an accumulation of chance occurrences and would soon lose all interest.

In return, another task that is no less interesting emerges: to reveal the unpredictable contours of this polygon, which no longer has the conventional forms or ample folds that make history into a noble tragedy, and to restore their original silhouette to events, which has been concealed under borrowed garments. The true forms are so irregular that they literally go unseen. Presuppositions "go without saying" and pass unnoticed, and in their place conventional generalities are seen. One notices neither the inquiry nor the controversy. One sees historical knowledge throughout the centuries and its progress. Greek criticism of myth becomes an episode in the progress of Reason, and Greek democracy would be eternal Democracy if it were not for the blot of slavery.

If, then, history proposes to lift the cloth and make what-goes-without-saying explicit, it ceases to be explanatory and becomes a hermeneutic.* Then we will not wonder what social causes lie at the root of the criticism of myth. In place of a kind of holy history of Enlightenment or Society we prefer to substitute a perpetual chance redistribution of ever-changing minor causes that engender effects no less due to chance but which pass for being great and revelatory of human purpose. Scheme for scheme, that of Pierre Bourdieu, which envisions the specificity and autonomy of the symbolic field as divided among centers of force, seems preferable to the scheme of social classes; two schemes are better than one.

Let us open here what will at first seem to be a parenthesis of several pages but which will in fact lead us to the heart of our problem of myth. If everything has to be said, we resign ourselves all the more easily to not explaining as we are led to think that the unpredictable nature of history is due less to its contingency (which would not prevent *post eventum* explanations) than to its capacity for invention. The idea brings on a smile, for everyone knows that it is mystical and antiscientific to believe in absolute beginnings. Thus it is annoying to note that scientific and explanatory thought rests, without our knowing it, on presuppositions that are no less arbitrary. Let us say it in a few words, for the use of those who, in public or private life, one fine morning find themselves doing or thinking things they never would have imagined the night before. And also for the use of those who have found themselves unable to predict the behavior of their most intimate friend but who, after the fact, have in retrospect discovered in this friend's past or character a trait that would have foretold it.

Nothing is simpler or more empirical in appearance than causality. Fire makes water boil; the rise of a new class brings about a new ideology. This apparent simplicity camouflages a complexity we are unaware of, a polarity between action and passivity. Fire is an agent that makes itself be obeyed; water is passive and does what the fire makes it do. In order to know what will happen, it is necessary to see in what direction the cause moves the effect; for the effect can no more

* to interpret, interpretative, to unfold the signification

innovate than a billiard ball can when it is struck and propelled by another. Same cause, same effect; causality will mean regular succession. The empirical interpretation of causality is no different. It abandons the anthropomorphism of a slave-like effect, regularly obeying the order of its cause, but it retains the essential part of the argument, the idea of regularity. Under the false sobriety of empiricism lurks a metaphor.

Now, since one metaphor is as good as another, one could as easily speak of fire and boiling or a rising class and its revolution in different terms, in which only active subjects operated. Then one would say that when an apparatus is assembled, comprising fire, a pot, water, and an infinity of other details, water "invents" boiling and will reinvent it each time it is put on the fire. As an agent, it responds to a situation; it actualizes a polygon of possibilities and deploys an activity that channels a polygon of tiny causes, which are obstacles limiting this energy more than they are motors. The metaphor is no longer that of a ball thrown in a specific direction but that of an elastic gas occupying the space left to it. It is no longer by considering "the" cause that we know what the gas will do; or rather, there is no longer any cause. The polygon does not permit the prediction of the future configuration of this expansion of energy; rather, it is the expansion of energy that reveals the polygon. This natural resiliency is also called the will to power.

If we lived in a society in which this metaphorical scheme operated, we would have no trouble admitting that a revolution, an intellectual fashion, a thrust of imperialism, or the success of a political system responds not to human nature, the needs of society, or the logic of things, but that this is a fashion, a project that we get stirred up about. Not only would it have been possible for the Revolution of 1789 not to have occurred (history being contingent), but, moreover, the bourgeoisie could have invented something else. In accordance with this dynamic and indeterminate scheme we would imagine the process of becoming as the more or less unpredictable work of exclusively active subjects that obey no law.

One could counter that this scheme is as unverifiable and metaphysical as the others, which are no less so, certainly; but it has the advantage of being an alternative solution that eliminates some false problems and frees our imagination. We were beginning to weary of the prison of social and ideological functionalism. One could equally object that if becoming comprises only active subjects, the causal regularities that reappear from time to time become incomprehensible. Not necessarily. If one unfailingly pits a heavyweight boxer against a featherweight, the heavier agent will regularly win. But let us suppose that, throughout the world, boxers are matched and paired off by chance. The regularities of such victories would cease to be the general rule, and boxing results would run the gamut from full predictability to complete irregularity to the stroke of genius. In this way we also account for the most obvious characteristic of historical transformation. It is composed of a spectrum of events that run from the most predictable and regular to the most unpredictable. Our theory of energy is a monism made up of chances—in other words, a pluralism. We will not make the Manichaean opposition between inertia and innovation, or between matter and the vital impulse, or other avatars of Good and Evil. The chance matching of unequal agents accounts as effectively for physical necessity as for radical innovation. Everything is invention or reinvention, one after the other.

In truth, the role of regular succession or reinvention is the effect of a *post eventum* analysis or even a retrospective illusion. Fire will explain boiling, and slippery streets will explain a frequent type of automobile accident—if we subtract all the other infinitely varied circumstances at work in these innumerable plots. Thus, historians and sociologists can never predict anything and can always be right. As Bergson writes in his admirable study on the possible and the real, the inventive nature of becoming is such that it is only by a retrospective illusion that the possible seems to exist prior to the real:

> How can we not see that if the event is always explained after the fact by such and such antecedent events, a completely different event would also be equally explained, in the same circumstances, by antecedents otherwise chosen—how to put it? by the same antecedents broken down, distributed, and perceived in a different way and, finally, by retrospective attention?

So let us not get too impassioned for or against the *post eventum* analysis of the causal structures among the student population of

* descent of deity to earth + his incarnation into a man or animal

Nanterre in April, 1968. In May of 1968 or July of 1789, if the revolutionaries had for some minor reason discovered a passion for a new religiosity, after the fact we would probably be able to find, in their *mentalité*, a means of making this fashion understandable. The simplest way is still to conveniently break down the event rather than the causes. If May of 1968 is an explosion of dissatisfaction with the administration (surrounded, alas, by a charade which, being exaggerated, does not truly exist), the true explanation of May, 1968, will assuredly be the poor administrative organization of the university system of the time.

Since Marx the spirit of seriousness has led us to consider historical or scientific becoming as a succession of problems that humanity poses for itself and resolves, while, obviously, acting or knowing humanity ceaselessly forgets each problem in order to think of something else. Thus a realistic approach would lie less in asking, "How will all this end?" than wondering, "What are they going to invent this time?" The existence of inventiveness means that history does not conform to schemes. Hitlerism was an invention in the sense that it is explained neither by eternal politics nor by the forces of production. It was an encounter among tiny causal series. The famous idea that "Facts do not exist" (the words are Nietzsche's and not Max Weber's) is not linked to the methodology of historical knowledge and the plurality of interpretations of the past made by different historians. It describes the structure of physical and human reality. Each fact (the relationships of production, "Power," "religious need," or social exigencies) plays a different role, or rather changes from one conjuncture to another. Its role and identity are only circumstantial.

Moreover, if one thing must surprise us, it is less the explanation of historical formations than their very existence. History is as complicated as it is inventive. What is man's capacity to actualize, for no reason and about nothing, these capacious constructions that go by the name of social and cultural works and practices and that are as complex and as unexpected as living species, as if man had energy he did not know what to do with?

Natural resiliency, or the will to power, explains a paradox known as the Tocqueville effect. Revolutions break out when an oppressive regime begins to become more liberal. Uprisings are not like a kettle that blows its lid off because it has begun to boil. On the contrary, it is a slight raising of the lid because of some external cause that brings the kettle to boil, and this succeeds in blowing off the lid.

This long parenthesis brings us to the heart of our theme: the flowering of myth and all manner of foolish tales ceases to mystify us by its gratuitousness and uselessness if we see that history itself is ceaseless invention and does not lead the reasonable life of a petty economizer. We have the habit of explaining events by a cause that moves the passive object in a predictable direction ("Guards, obey me!''); but since the future remains unforeseeable, we are resigned to the composite solution of mixing intelligibility with contingency. A tiny pebble can jam or throw the moving body off course, the guard can fail to obey (and, if they had obeyed, writes Trotsky, there would have been no revolution in Leningrad in February, 1917), and the revolution can fail to break out (and, Trotsky also writes, if Lenin had had a tiny stone in his bladder, the revolution of October, 1917, would not have begun). Pebbles so minute that they have neither the dignity of intelligible schemes nor the weight needed to disqualify them.

But suppose that, instead of a cause, corrected by contingency, we have elasticity and a polygon with an indefinite number of sides (for often the sides will be counted in the retrospective light of the event). The resulting event is active. Like a gas, it occupies all the space left free between the causes, and it occupies them rather then not occupying them. History expends itself for nothing and fails to meet its own needs. The possibility of predicting will depend on the configuration of each polygon and will always be limited; for we can never account for an in(de)finite number of sides of which no one is more determinative than the others. The dualism of intelligibility corrected by the admission of contingency disappears or, rather, is replaced by contingency in a different sense, one that is truly richer than that of Cleopatra's nose: the negation of a prime mover of history (such as the relationship of production, Politics, the will to power) and the affirmation of the plurality of movers (we would say instead, the plurality of these obstacles that are the sides of the polygon). A thousand tiny causes take the place of a single intelligibility. It disappears as well, because a polygon is not a scheme. No longer is there any transhistorical scheme of revolution or social preferences in literature or cuisine. Henceforth, every event resembles, more or less, an unpredictable invention. Elucidating this event will be more interesting than enumerating its minute causes, and it will in any case be the preliminary task. Finally, if everything is history, and if there are as many different polygons as there are revolutions, what remains for the human sciences to talk about? What then could they tell us about Greek myth that history could not teach us?

4
Social Diversity of Beliefs and Mental Balkanization

One does not know what one does not have the right to ask (whence the sincere blindness of so many husbands and parents), and one does not doubt what others believe, if they are respected. Relationships among truths are relationships of force. This is the root of what is called bad faith.

The Greeks distinguished between two domains: gods and heroes. For they did not understand myth or the mythmaking function in a general way but evaluated myths according to content. Criticism of the heroic generations consisted in transforming heroes into simple men and giving them a past that matched that of what were called the human generations, that is, history since the Trojan War. The first step of this criticism was to remove the visible intervention of the gods from history. Not that the very existence of these gods was doubted in the least. But in our day the gods most often remain invisible to men. This was already the case even before the Trojan War, and the whole of the Homeric supernatural is nothing but invention and credulity. Criticism of religious beliefs indeed existed, but it was very different. Some thinkers purely and simply denied either the existence of a particular god or, perhaps, the existence of any of the gods in which the people believed. On the other hand, the immense majority of philosophers, as well as educated people, did not so much criticize the gods as seek an idea worthy of divine majesty. Religious criticism consisted in saving the idea of the gods by purifying it of all superstition, and the criticism of heroic myths saved the heroes by making them as probable and lifelike as simple men.

The two critical attitudes operated independently, and the most pious minds would have been the first to remove from the so-called heroic epoch the childish interventions, miracles, and battles of the gods that Homer presents in the *Iliad*. No one thought of stamping out

Infamy* and transforming the criticism of heroes into a war machine or guerilla attack of allusions against religion. This is the paradox: there were people who did not believe in the existence of the gods, but never did anyone doubt the existence of the heroes. And with reason: the heroes were only men, to whom credulity had lent supernatural traits, and how could one doubt that human beings now exist and have always existed? Not everyone, on the other hand, was disposed to believe in the reality of the gods, for no one could see them with his own eyes. As a result, during the period that we are going to study, which extends for almost a millennium, from the fifth century B.C to the fourth century A.D., absolutely no one, Christians included, ever expressed the slightest doubt concerning the historicity of Aeneas, Romulus, Theseus, Heracles, Achilles, or even Dionysus; rather, everyone asserted this historicity. Later on we will shed some light on the presuppositions governing this long-standing belief. First we will describe which Greeks believed in what throughout these nine centuries.

A mass of folkloric superstitions, which sometimes also were found in what was already called mythology, existed among the populace. Among the educated classes this mythology found entire acceptance, as much as it did in Pindar's day; the general public believed in the reality of Centaurs and accepted the legend of Heracles or Dionysus with an uncritical spirit. The same naïveté will be found among the readers of the *Golden Legend,* and for the same reasons. They will believe in the miracles of Saint Nicholas and the legend of Saint Catherine (this "papist Minerva," as the Protestants will call her) because they are docile when faced with another's word, because they lack any way to systematize daily experience, and because they are possessed of a respectful and virtuous mentality. Lastly, the learned formulated historical criticism of the myths with the success with which we are already familiar. The sociologically odd result is this: the ingenuousness of the people and the criticism of the learned did not go to war for the triumph of Reason, nor was the former culturally devalued. It followed that each individual, if he belonged to the ranks

---

*The French reads "nul ne songeait à écraser l'Infâme. . . ." The reference is to Voltaire's famous slogan, *Ecrasez l'infâme!,* "Crush the wretched thing!"—the "wretched thing" being religion, which he viewed as a source of superstition, ignorance, intolerance, and fanaticism.

of the learned, internalized something of a peaceful coexistence in the field of relations of symbolic force, which resulted in half-beliefs, hesitations, and contradictions, on the one hand, and, on the other, the possibility of juggling different levels of meaning. It was from the latter, in particular, that an "ideological"—or, rather, rhetorical—use of mythology emerged.

In Petronius' *Satyricon,* a naïve rich parvenu says that he saw with his own eyes a Sibyl magically miniaturized and enclosed in a bottle, as is told of the genie in the *Arabian Nights.* In Menander's *Bad-Tempered Man* a misanthrope would pay a great deal to possess the magical objects of the hero Perseus: the helmet that made him invisible and the mask of Medusa that permitted him to transform troublesome people into statues. He is not speaking figuratively; he believes in all these wonders. In the same period, the learned of the higher social class, who were famous writers, such as Pliny the Younger, wondered if one should believe in ghosts as seriously, they tell me, as people asked the same question in the England of Shakespeare's day.

It cannot be doubted that the Greeks believed in their mythology for as long a time as their nurses or mothers told them such tales. "That Theseus treated Ariadne unjustly . . . when he abandoned her while asleep on the island of Dia, you must have heard from your nurse; for these women are skilled in telling such tales and they weep over them whenever they will. I do not need to say to you that it is Theseus you see on the ship and Dionysus yonder on the land. . . ."[56] We will thus propose that "legendary belief is the acceptance of inauthentic and invented myths, such as those relative to Cronos, among others; as a matter of fact, many believe this."[57]

But which myths did nurses tell children? They certainly spoke to them of the gods, for piety and superstition required it. They frightened them with boogeymen and Lamias; they told them sentimental stories about Ariadne or Psyche for their own amusement, and they wept. But did they teach the children the great mythic cycles: those of Thebes, Oedipus, the Argonauts? Did not the little boy, and the little girl as well,[58] have to wait until they were under the grammarian's authority to learn the great legends?[59]

A word must be said about a famous but still little-studied work, the *Heroicus* by Philostratus. It is a difficult text, for as is often the case in the Second Sophistic, its style, fantasy, and antiquarian and patriotic

✗ person who has risen by acquisition of wealth 43
above the station in which he was born – usually
derogatory.

ideology are blended with contemporary reality. Philostratus meets a poor peasant, who cultivates a vineyard not far from the tomb of the hero Protesilaus.[60] The grape-grower leaves part of his land fallow (he tills his land himself and took it away from his slaves, who failed to bring in enough), because these fields were consecrated to the hero Protesilaus by the preceding landowner, to whom the hero's ghost had appeared. This phantom continues to appear to our vine-grower and to the peasants of the area, as do the ghosts of the Achaeans who had gone off with Protesilaus to beseige Troy. Sometimes their plumed shadows can be seen moving on the plain. Far from frightening the people, the hero's ghost is well loved. He gives the farmers advice, is an omen of rain and fine weather. The people of the region address their prayers to this hero and scribble them on the statue, now shapeless, that stands above his tomb, for Protesilaus cures all ailments.[61] He also encourages the undertakings of lovers seeking the favors of an adolescent. On the other hand, he is pitiless toward adulterers, for he has a moral sense. As we see, this story of a hero's cult is also a ghost story.[62] The rest of the dialogue is a Homeric fantasy in the manner of the time, in which the farmer reveals a mass of unknown details concerning the Trojan War and its heroes. He gets them from his friend Protesilaus in person. This part of the dialogue is the longest and the most important in the eyes of Philostratus. We have the impression that the author knew of the existence of some peasant superstitition concerning an old rustic temple and that he linked it to mythology, which by now has become classical and bookish. In this way he plunges his readers, his compatriots, into an ageless Hellenism that could belong to Lucian or Longus, or into an eternal Greece, so dear to the nationalistic classicism of his day, in which Hellenistic patriotism was a reaction against Roman domination. It is certain that the peasants who served as his models knew nothing of the Trojan War. It is easy to believe that their naïve cult centered on an old tomb of Protesilaus; but what did they know of the hero they still called by this name?

The people had their legends, in which certain myths were mentioned. There were also heroes, such as Heracles, whose name and nature—if not the details of his adventures—everyone knew. Other purely classical legends were known through songs.[63] In any case, oral literature and iconography made the existence and fictional modality of a mythological world familiar to all, even if not all the details were familiar. Only those who had attended school knew the fine points. But, in a slightly different way, has this not always been the case? Do we really believe that classical Athens was a great civic collectivity where all minds acted in concert, where the theater ratified the union among hearts, and where the average citizen could pass any test about Jocasta or the return of the Heraclidae?

The essence of a myth is not that everyone knows it but that it is supposed to be known and is worthy of being known by all. Furthermore, it was not generally known. A revealing phrase occurs in the *Poetics*.[64] One is not obliged, says Aristotle, to restrict oneself to hallowed myths if one writes a tragedy: "It would be absurd, in fact, to do so, as even the known stories are known to only a few, though they are a delight none the less to all." In a general way the Athenian public were aware of the existence of the mythical world in which tragedies took place, but they did not know the details of the stories. Nor did they need to know the fine points of the Oedipus legend in order to follow *Antigone* or *The Phoenicians*. The tragic poet took care to reveal everything to his audience, just as if he had invented his plot. But the poet did not place himself above his public, since myth was supposed to be known. He did not know any more about it than they did. He was not writing learned literature.

All of this changes in the Hellenistic period. Literature is intended to be learned. Not that this is the first time that literature has been reserved for an elite (Pindar or Aeschylus were not exactly popular writers), but it demands a cultural effort from its audience that excludes the amateurs. Myths then give way to what we still call mythology and which will survive until the eighteenth century. The people continued to have their tales and superstitions, but mythology, now a matter for the learned, moved beyond their reach. It took on the prestige of the elite knowledge that marks its possessor as belonging to a certain class.[65]

During the Hellenistic period, when literature became a specific activity that authors and readers cultivated for its own sake, mythology became a discipline that soon would be studied in school. This does not mean that mythology dies—quite the contrary, in fact. It remains one of the great elements of culture and never ceases to be a stumbling block for the literate. Callimachus gathered rare variants of the great legends and local myths, not out of frivolity (nothing is less frivolous than Alexandrianism), but patriotic piety. It has even been supposed that he and his disciples traveled the Greek world with the deliberate intention of collecting such legends.[66] Four centuries later, Pausanias traveled throughout Greece and combed the libraries with the same passion. Once it had become a matter for books, mythology would continue to grow, but what was published was garbed in the taste of the day. The new literature presented legends for entertainment and exhibited a predilection for metamorphoses and catasterisms.[67] The taste for the latter continued to flourish in the time of Catullus, the *Ciris,* and Ovid. In a word, by the grace of the grammarians and rhetoricians, Myth is put into manuals, thereby undergoing a codification that will simplify it and cast the great cycles as official versions and strand the variants in oblivion. It is this learned vulgate, meant to serve the study of classical authors, that constitutes the mythology familiar to a Lucian. It is the mythology that will be taught to the young scholars of classical Europe. The serious side of the matter still remained: What was one to think of this mass of tales? Here there are two schools, which we wrongly conflate in the too-modern term the "rational treatment of myth." On the one hand were the believers, such as Diodorus, but also Euhemerus; on the other were the learned.

Indeed, there existed a believing but educated public that demanded a new type of supernatural, which must no longer be situated, beyond matters of truth and falsehood, in an ageless past. It was to be "scientific" or, rather, historical. For it was no longer possible to believe in the supernatural in the old way. The reason for this shift is not, I believe, to be found in the Sophistic *Aufklärung* but in the success of the historical genre. To be accepted, myth must henceforth pass for history, and this mystification then takes on the deceptive appearance of a rationalization. This transmutation produces the falsely contradictory aspect of Timaeus, one of the great purveyors of the genre. He wrote a history "full of dreams, prodigies, incredible tales, and, to put it shortly, craven superstition and womanish love of the marvellous."[68] The same Timaeus gives myths a rational interpretation.

Many historians, writes Diodorus, have "avoided as a difficulty the history of fabulous times."[69] He is intent on filling this gap himself. Zeus was a king, the son of a certain Cronos, who himself reigned over the entire West. This Zeus was truly the master of the world. This Zeus should not be confused with one of his homonyms, who was only the king of Crete and who had two sons, called the Couretes.[70] This is the same Diodorus[71] who, one hundred pages later, accepts as common currency the imaginary voyages of Euhemerus through wondrous islands, one of which had for kings Ouranos, Cronos, and Zeus, who were divinized for their benefactions, as the inscriptions engraved in the language of their country prove and who are taken as gods "at home." Did Euhemerus disguise some enterprise of religious or even political demystification in the form of a tale? Or rather, does he not wish to give his readers modern reasons to believe in myth and the marvelous? People had a relaxed attitude toward storytellers. No great importance was accorded the myths found in the works of the historians, even if they did not admit to writing myths; for, as Strabo says, we know that they had no other intent than to entertain and astonish by means of an invented supernatural.[72] However, the marvelous of the Hellenistic period has a rationalist cast, so that the moderns are mistakenly tempted to see in it a battle for truth and enlightenment.

In fact, there were readers for whom the need for truth obtained and others for whom it was not a factor. A passage from Diodorus acquaints us with the case. It is difficult, says this historian, to narrate the history of mythical times, if only because of the imprecision of the chronology. Such inexactness makes it impossible for many readers to take mythical history seriously.[73] Furthermore, the events of this distant time are too far away and too unlikely to be readily believed.[74] What can be done? The exploits of Heracles are as glorious as they are superhuman.

> A writer is under the necessity either of omitting the greatest deeds and so detracting somewhat from the fame of the god, or of recounting them all and in so doing making the history of them incredible. For some readers set up an unfair standard and require in the accounts of the ancient myths the same exactness as in the events of our own time . . . and estimate the might of Heracles by the weakness of the men of our day.

These readers who apply the false principle of current things to Heracles are also mistaken in wanting things to happen on the stage as they do in real life. And this is to show a lack of respect for the heroes:

> When the histories of myths are concerned, a man should by
> no means scrutinize the truth with so sharp an eye. In the
> theatres, for instance, though we are persuaded there have
> existed no Centaurs who are composed of two different kinds
> of bodies nor any Geryones with three bodies, yet we look
> with favour upon such products of the myths as these, and by
> our applause we enhance the honour of the god. And strange
> it would be indeed that Heracles, while yet among mortal
> men, should by his own labours have brought under
> cultivation the inhabited world, and that human beings
> should nevertheless forget the benefactions which he
> rendered them generally and slander the commendation he
> receives for the noblest deeds.

The test is revealing in its adroit ingenuousness. We can sense here the uneasy coexistence of two programs of truth, one of which is critical, the other respectful.[75] The conflict had drawn the partisans of the second away from spontaneity to fidelity to oneself. Henceforth they had "convictions" and demanded respect for them. The notion of truth faded into the background; disrespect was scandalous, and what was scandalous was therefore false. Since every good was also true, only what was good was true. Diodorus, who plays to his audience, here becomes a one-man band. He manages to see things with the eyes of those in one camp and then the other camp, to give right-thinking people the impression that he reconciles the critics' viewpoints for them, and, finally, to place himself on the side of the orthodox. He seems to show bad faith because he expresses the respectful belief of the first in the critical language of the second. This at least proves that the believers were always numerous. In their modernized versions, Heracles and Bacchus were no longer divine figures but gods who were men or divine men, to whom humanity owed civilization. And, in fact, from time to time a sensational incident revealed that the crowd and the elites continued to believe in this half-divine supernatural.[76]

Testimonies converge. The majority of the public believed the legends about Cronos, says Sextus Empiricus. They believe what the tragedies say about Prometheus, Niobe, and Theseus, write Artemidorus and Pausanias. Why not? The learned, too, believed in Theseus; the populace was limited because it did not purify the myth. Just as in the archaic period, the human past was seen to be preceded by a wondrous period that formed another world, real in itself and unreal in relation to our own. When a character from Plautus, short on funds, states, "I will pray to Achilles to give me the gold that he received for Hector's ransom," he is jokingly indicating the most fantastic way possible of procuring gold.[77]

In this civilization, nothing was seen beyond a nearby temporal horizon. People wondered with Epicurus whether the world was a thousand years old or two, no more, or, with Aristotle and Plato, whether it was not eternal but ravaged by periodic catastrophes, after each of which everything began again as before—which came down to thinking like Epicurus. Since the life-rhythm of our world is so short, the world could traverse considerable evolutions: the Homeric period and the heroic generations constituted Antiquity in the eyes of this ancient civilization. When Virgil wishes to depict archaic Carthage as it must have been eleven centuries before his own time, he gives it a Homeric character. Nothing could be less Flaubertian than Dido's city. . . .

Already Herodotus was opposing the heroic to the human generations. Much later, when Cicero wants to be charmed by a philosophical dream of immortality and gives it the character of an idyll in the Elysian fields, he takes pleasure in thinking that in these meadows, where learned discourse abounds, his soul will converse with that of the wise Ulysses or the sagacious Sisyphus.[78] If Cicero's reverie had been less magical, he would have promised himself instead to speak with the figures of Roman history: Scipio, Cato, or Marcellus, whose memory he evokes four pages later. A scholar of the same era had given these problems a didactic clarity. According to Varro, the obscure age stretched from Deucalion to the Flood; from the Flood to the first Olympiad (where chronology becomes certain) was the mythical age, "so called because it contains many fables"; from the first Olympiad, in 776 B.C., to the time of Varro and Cicero, stretches the historical age, where "events are recorded in truthful history books."[79]

The learned, we see, are not easily deceived; but by a first paradox they doubt the gods much more easily than they do the heroes. For example, Cicero: in politics or ethics he is perceptibly the equal of Victor Cousin, and he is quite capable of believing in what agrees with his interests. On the other hand, he has a religiously cold temperament, and in this area is is incapable of professing something that he does not believe. Any reader of his treatise on the nature of the gods will agree that he does not believe in the latter very much and that he does not even try to make a different impression for the sake of political expediency. He lets it appear that in his day, as in our own, individuals were divided on matters of religion. Did Castor and Pollux really appear to a certain Vatienus on a road outside Rome? The question was discussed among the devout of the old school and the skeptics.[80] Opinions were also divided concerning myth. According to Cicero, the friendship of Theseus and Pirithous and their descent into Hell are only an invention, a *fabula ficta*. We will spare the reader the requisite considerations on class interest in religion and mythology. Now the same Cicero, who believes neither in the appearance of Castor and his brother nor, undoubtedly, in their very existence, and who does not hide it, fully admits the historicity of Aeneas and Romulus. Furthermore, no one was to question this historicity until the nineteenth century.

Here is a second paradox: almost everything that is told about these characters is only an empty tale, but the total of these zeroes makes a positive sum. Theseus indeed existed. Cicero, from the first page of his *De Legibus,* pleasantly jests about Romulus' supposed apparition after his death and about good king Numa's conversations with his nymph Egeria. In his *Republic* he does not believe that Romulus was the son of a god who had impregnated a Vestal Virgin, either: a venerable tale, but a tale nonetheless.[81] Nor does he believe in the apotheosis of the founder of Rome; the posthumous divinization of Romulus is but a legend fit for naïve times. Nevertheless, Romulus is a historically authentic person, and, according to Cicero, what is strange about his divinization is precisely that it had been invented in the middle of the historic age, for it takes place after the seventh Olympiad. In the matters of Romulus and Numa, Cicero questions everything except their very existence. To be precise, a third paradox appears here. Sometimes the learned seem very skeptical about myth as a whole and consign it to oblivion with a few well-chosen words. At others, they seem once again to have become completely credulous. This restoration of belief happens each time that, confronted with a given episode, they wish to be serious and responsible thinkers. Is this bad faith or half-belief? Neither. Instead, they are wavering between two criteria of the truth, one of which requires the rejection of the marvelous, the other the persuasion that it is impossible to create a gratuitous lie.

Is myth true or false? It is suspect, hence their ill-humored gesture. These fables are nothing but old wives' tales. Different cities, writes a rhetorician, owe their origins either to some god or hero or to the man who founded it.[82] "Of these different etiologies, those which are divine or heroic are legendary [*mythōdes*], and those which are human are more worthy of belief." Since the archaic period the value of the word "myth" has shifted. For example, when an author no longer frames a tale as his own but puts it in indirect discourse, "A myth says that . . . ," he is no longer claiming to make a bit of information, floating in the air, well known to all. He is withdrawing from the game and letting each one think what he pleases. "Myth" has become a slightly pejorative term, describing a suspect tradition.

A text is marked by a date. One day Isocrates[83] felt the need to virtuously protest that a legend found no unbelievers. "Zeus," he writes, "engendered Heracles and Tantalus, as the myths say and everyone believes." This clumsy zeal betrays a certain bad conscience. No longer knowing what to think, the historian Ephorus begins his history only at the point of the return of the Heraclidae[84] and refuses to go back any further. To our eyes this still comprises a goodly slice of the legendary past. Did Ephorus reject the older tales as false? Is it to be believed instead that he had abandoned the attempt to find the truth in them and preferred to abstain from comment? Indeed, it was painfully necessary for him to abandon the ancient historians' tendency to accept the entire tradition in one piece, like a vulgate.

Ephorus will refrain from stating his approval, but he and his peers will also refrain from offering any condemnation. And here begins the second movement we mentioned: the return to credulity by means of methodical criticism. A true background lies behind every legend. Consequently, when the historians move from the totality, which is suspect, to the detail and to individual myths, they once again become cautious. They question myths as a group, but not a one of them denies the historicity forming the basis of any legend. The moment it is no longer a question of expressing his overall doubt but offering a verdict on a specific point and engaging his word as a serious scholar, the historian begins to believe again. He clings to the task of sorting and safeguarding the true kernel.

We have to be careful here. When Cicero in his *De re publica* and Titus Livy in his preface admit that the events "before Rome was born or thought of" are known only "in the form of old tales with more the charm of poetry than of a sound historical record," they are not offering a glimpse of modern historical criticism or foreshadowing Beaufort, Niebuhr, and Dumézil. They are not condemning the general uncertainty about the four centuries following the city's foundation and the absence of any contemporaneous documents. They are complaining that the documents related to an even older period are not certain. For these documents exist. They are traditions, but they are suspect, not because they date from a time long after the fact but because credulity has entered into the matter. What Livy and Cicero refuse to support is the divine birth of Romulus or the miracle of Aeneas' ships transformed into nymphs.

Knowledge of legendary times, then, emerges from a mode of knowledge that is completely habitual to us but made the Ancients uncomfortable when it was applied to history: criticism, conjectural knowledge, and scientific hypothesis. Speculation, *eikasia,* replaces confidence in tradition. It will be based on the notion that the past resembles the present. This had been the foundation on which Thucydides, seeking to know more than tradition, had already built his brilliant but perfectly false and gratuitous reconstruction of the first days of Greece.

Since this principle makes it equally possible to purify myth of its portion of the marvelous, it becomes possible to believe in all legends, which is what the greatest minds of this very great period did. Aristotle, for example, is master of his words, and when he means, "People say that . . ." or "according to what people believe," he says it. He distinguishes between myth and what is not mythical.[85] Now, we have seen him accept the historicity of Theseus and give a rational version of the story of the Minotaur.[86] Thucydides, who did not question the historicity of Minos, either, also believed in the historical reality of Hellen, ancient king of the Hellenes, and reconstructed the true political roles played by Itys, Pandion, Procne, and Philomela (who, according to legend, were transformed into birds).[87] He refuses, on the other hand, to provide explanations concerning the Cyclopes and the monstrous Laestrygones, for everyone thinks what they will about them or believes what the poets say![88] For it is one thing to believe that in the past there were already kings and another entirely to believe that there were monsters, which no longer exist. The principles governing the criticism of traditions that would obtain for the next millennium were in place; they were already there with Plato.[89] So Strabo, as befits a scholar, can separate the true from the false. Dionysus and Heracles existed; they were great travelers and geographers; and so legend claimed that they had triumphantly covered the entire earth. Odysseus existed but did not make all the voyages that Homer attributed to him, for the poet had used this ploy to teach his listeners useful geographical details. As for Jason, the ship Argo, and Aeëtes, these are "things that are agreed upon by everybody," and, up to that point, "Homer tells his story, agreeing . . . with matters of history." Fiction begins when the poet claims that the Argonauts reached the Ocean. Other great voyagers, Theseus and Pirithous, explored so much of the world that legend claimed that they had gone as far as Hell.[90]

Nonconformist minds reasoned no differently than this Stoic geographer. For the Epicurean Lucretius, a great enemy of fables, the wars of Troy and Thebes brook no doubt; they are the oldest known events.[91] Let us end with the great Polybius.[92] When he is in the presence of an official version, he gives it without any commentary: "Their [the Achaeans'] first king was Tisamenus the son of Orestes, who [was] expelled from Sparta on the return of the Heraclidae." When he offers a negligible myth, he keeps his distance. A particular hamlet in the country of the Achaeans was "fabled to have been built long ago by Heracles." But, when he shoulders his responsibility as a historian, he applies tested critical methods to myths, and he can propose that

> Aeolus indicated the direction to take in the strait of Messina, there where a double current makes the passage difficult because of the tide; thus it has been said that he was the administrator of the winds, he was taken for the king of the wind. In the same manner, Danaus, who taught the technique of making cisterns that is seen in Argos, or Atreus, who taught the retrograde movement of the sun, are described as kings, sorcerers, augurs.

Earlier the object of naïve credulity, hesitant skepticism, and daring speculations, myth is now treated with a thousand precautions. But these precautions are very calculated. When filling out the contours of some legend, the writers of the Hellenistic and Roman periods seem to hesitate. They often refuse to speak in their own name. "People say . . . ," they write, or "according to myth." But in the next sentence they will be very definite concerning another point of the same legend. These shifts between daring and reserve owe nothing to chance. They follow three rules: state no opinion on the marvelous and the supernatural, admit a historical basis, and take exception to the details. One example will suffice. Narrating Pompey's flight toward Brinidisi and Durazzo after Caesar had crossed the Rubicon, Appian speaks of the origins of the town of Durazzo, the ancient Dyrrachium, on the Ionian Sea. The town owes its name to Dyrrachus, the son of a princess "and," people say, "of Neptune." This Dyrrachus, states Appian, "had Hercules as an ally" in a war that he waged against his brothers, the princes, and this is why the hero is honored as a god by the people of the regions. These natives "say that during the battle Hercules mistakenly killed Ion, his ally Dyrrachus' own son, and that he threw the body into the sea so that this sea would take the name of the unfortunate one." Appian believes in Hercules and the war, rejects Neptune's paternity, and gives the locals credit for an anecdote.

Among the learned, critical credulity, as it were, alternated with a global skepticism and rubbed shoulders with the unreflecting credulity of the less educated. These three attitudes tolerated one another, and popular credulity was not culturally devalued. This peaceful coexistence of contradictory beliefs had a sociologically peculiar result. Each individual internalized the contradiction and thought things about myth that, in the eyes of a logician at least, were irreconcilable. The individual himself did not suffer from these contradictions; quite the contrary. Each one served a different end.

Take for example a philosophical mind of the first order, the physician Galen.[93] Did he, or did he not, believe in the reality of Centaurs? It depends.

When he is speaking as a scholar and laying out his personal theories, he speaks of the Centaurs in terms that imply that for himself and his most select readers these marvelous beings had barely any present reality. Medicine, he says, teaches reasonable knowledge, or "theorems," and the first condition of a good theorem is that it be perceivable by the senses. "For, if the theorem is unrealizable, in the manner of the following statement, *The centaur's bile relieves apoplexy,* it is useless because it escapes our apperception." There are no Centaurs, or at least no one has ever seen one.

Centaurs belonged to a supernatural bestiary that equaled that of our Middle Ages, and one suspects that the reality of this bestiary was a subject of difficulty or irritation. Galen finds childish the seriousness with which the Stoics examined poetic fictions and their toiling to give an allegorical meaning to everything the poets say of the gods. Pursuing such a goal, he adds, imitating Plato, one will go so far as to "correct the idea of Centaurs, Chimaeras, and then the throng of Gorgons and Pegasus and other impossible and absurd beings of this sort will be loosed. If in the name of a somewhat rustic wisdom one tries to make them probable without believing in their reality, one will go to a good deal of trouble for nothing." If no one in Galen's time had ever taken the legend of the Centaurs literally, why would the philosophers have needed to speak seriously of these things and reduce them to mere likelihood? If no one had believed in them, why would Galen himself have had to deliberately distinguish between those who did and did not believe in them? Moreover, Galen, in his great book on the finality of the parts of the organism, fights for a long time the idea that mixed natures, such as the Centaurs, could exist. He could not have done this without ridicule if Centaurs did not have their believers.

But when the same Galen no longer seeks to impose his ideas but to win new disciples, he seems to pass to the side of the believers. Summarizing his whole view of medicine in one hundred pages and determined to give the most lofty idea of this science, he offers an account of its high origin: the Greeks, he says, attribute the discovery of the different arts to the sons of the gods or to their familiars. Apollo taught medicine to his son Asclepius. Before him, men had only a limited experience with some remedies, herbals, "and, in Greece lay therein, for example, all the knowledge of the centaur Chiron and the heroes of whom he was the teacher."

This historical role accorded to a centaur is assuredly only pompous, conventional language. It is certainly what Antiquity called rhetoric, and rhetoric was the art of winning more than the art of being right. In order to win—that is, to convince—it was doubtless necessary to start with what people thought rather than to rub the jury the wrong way by telling them that they were mistaken on everything and must change their worldview to acquit the accused. Paris is worth a Mass, and one more disciple is worth a centaur. Only it would be specious to place rhetoric as an interested attitude in opposition to philosophy. This is not to say that rhetoric is not without philosophical dignity. I mean quite the contrary: that philosophy and truth both operate on the basis of interests. It is not true that, when they have a motive, intellectuals must be lying and that they are disinterested when they tell the truth. Galen had every reason to tell the truth about centaurs and deny their existence when his interest lay in the victory of his personal ideas among his disciples rather than in the recruiting of new ones. Exploring minds have different aims and tactics, depending on the circumstances. We are all in the same situation, even if we, and our disciples with us, take our jealousies to be righteous indignation and make a lofty idea of our scientific and ethical disinterest. We wage war for what Jean-Claude Passeron calls the division of the symbolic steak, and our politics are as diverse as those of nations and factions: to maintain position, launch an alliance or a league for conquest, reign without governing, establish the *pax Romana,* carve out an empire, defend one's own plot of land, seek virgin territory, have a Monroe Doctrine, or weave a net of public relations in order to control a group for mutual aid.

But since this politics of ideas is often unconscious, it is internalized. It is difficult, for example, not to begin to believe a little in the foreign dogmas against which one has formed an offensive or defensive confederacy. For we line up our beliefs in accordance with our words, so that we end up no longer knowing what we truly think. When he was relying on popular belief in centaurs, Galen, for want of cynicism, must have been caught up in a whirl of noble and indulgent verbiage and no longer knew too well what he thought of it all. In such a moment are born these modalities of wavering belief, this capacity to simultaneously believe in incompatible truths, which is the mark of times of intellectual confusion. The Balkanization of the symbolic field is reflected in each mind. This confusion corresponds to a sectarian politics of alliance. Regarding myth, the Greeks lived for a thousand years in this state. The moment an individual wishes to convince and be recognized, he must respect different ideas, if they are forces, and must partake of them a little. Now we know that the learned respected popular ideas on myth and that they themselves were split between two principles: the rejection of the marvelous and the conviction that legends had a true basis. Hence their complicated state of mind.

Aristotle and Polybius, so defiant when they are confronting Myth, did not believe in the historicity of Theseus or Aeolus, king of the wind, out of conformity or political calculation. Nor did they seek to challenge myths, but only to rectify them. Why rectify them? Because nothing that does not presently exist is worthy of belief. But then, why not challenge it all? Because the Greeks never admitted that the mythmaking process could lie to everyone about everything. The ancient problematic of myth, as we will see, is bounded by two dogmas that were unconscious, for they were self-evident. It was impossible to lie gratuitously, or lie about everything to everyone, for knowledge is only a mirror; and the mirror blends with what it reflects, so that the medium is not distinguished from the message.

5
Behind This Sociology an Implicit Program of Truth

Relationships of force, whether symbolic or not, are not invariable. They undoubtedly have the arbitrariness of analogical formations, but different ones. Their transhistorical appearance is an analogical illusion. Their sociology is set within the limits of an arbitrary and historical program.

Criticizing myths did not mean proving they were false but rediscovering their truthful basis. For this truth had been overlaid with lies. "All through the ages, many events that have occurred in the past, and even some that occur today, have been generally discredited because of the lies built up on a foundation of fact. . . . Those who like to listen to the miraculous are themselves apt to add to the marvel, and so they ruin truth by mixing it with falsehood."[94] But where do these lies come from, and what purpose do they serve? This is something the Greeks did not wonder about a great deal, since a lie has nothing positive about it. It is nonbeing, and that is all. They hardly wondered why some had lied; instead, they wondered why others had believed. It is with the moderns, from Fontenelle to Cassirer, Bergson, and Lévi-Strauss, that the problem of myth becomes that of its genesis. For the Greeks, this genesis did not pose any problems. At bottom, myths are authentic historical traditions, for how could one speak of what does not exist? The truth can be altered, but it is impossible to speak of nothing. On this point the moderns wonder instead whether one is able to speak without a motive, without some interest being involved. Even Bergson, who developed the idea of gratuitous mythmaking to its fullest, postulates first that storytelling initially has a vital function;[95] only this function goes awry and often turns to nothing. Fontenelle was doubtless the first one to say it: myths have no basis in truth and are not even allegories. "Therefore let us not seek anything else in fable but the history of the errors of the human spirit."[96]

The Greeks sought a truth behind the lies. They asked what was the cause—ingenuousness, naïveté, *euētheia*—for such was the sanctioned term.[97] It is ingenuousness that leads one to place one's faith in "what in the historical depths has been tainted with falsity,"[98] and these falsities, mixed with myth, are called the *mythōdes*.[99] It is truly naïveté that is responsible for lies. There would be fewer storytellers if there were fewer naïve listeners.[100] The *antiqua credulitas* explains that most myths date back to ancient times.[101] Myth is an account of true events covered with the accretion of legends that have multiplied over time. The older a tradition is, the more the *mythōdes* encumbers it and renders it less worthy of belief.[102]

For the moderns, on the contrary, myth will be the narration of a great event, and it is this that gives rise to its legendary aspect. This event is less altered by adventitious elements than it is epically magnified. For the popular soul enlarges great national exploits. Legend has its origin in the popular genius, which makes up stories to tell what is really true. That which is most true in legends is precisely the marvelous; that is where the emotion of the national soul is revealed. Rightly or wrongly, ancients and moderns believe in the historicity of the Trojan War—but for the opposite reasons. We believe because of its marvelous aspect; they believed in spite of it. For the Greeks, the Trojan War had existed because a war has nothing of the marvelous about it; if one takes the marvelous out of Homer, this war remains. For the moderns, the Trojan War is true because of the fabulous elements with which Homer surrounds it: only an authentic event that moved the national soul gives birth to epic and legend.

For the Greeks a mythic tradition is true *despite* the marvelous. Origen says it very well: historic events cannot be subject to logical proof even when they are authentic.[103] For example, it would be impossible to demonstrate that the Trojan War truly took place if someone denied it on the grounds that the account of this war contains certain unlikely details, to wit: that Achilles was the son of a goddess, Aeneas the son of Aphrodite, and Sarpedon the son of Zeus. The demonstration would be all the more difficult because we would be hampered by "the fictitious stories which for some unknown reason are bound up with the opinion, which everyone believes, that there really was a war in Troy.'' Let us suppose again, continues Origen, that someone ''does not believe the story about Oedipus and Jocasta, and Eteocles and Polyneices, sons of them both, because the half-maiden Sphinx is bound up with it. Proof is immediately impossible. The same will be said of the Epigones, even though their story contains no fictitious elements, and of the return of the Heraclidae, as well as of a thousand other stories.'' Myths therefore have a true basis, and if the historicity of the wars of Troy and Thebes, recognized by all, is not demonstrable, it is because no event can be proved.

But then, if along with the lies, myth contains some truth, the most urgent task is not to psychologize the storyteller but to learn how to be alert to falsehood. The victim is more interesting than the guilty party. The Greeks always thought that the human sciences were normative rather than descriptive, or, rather, they never even thought to make a distinction.[104] In their eyes a science of myth would not undertake to elucidate the error but to learn how to beware of it. Instead of asking whether myth explains ritual, or reveals through its structure the structure of the human mind, or is a functional or disordered creativity, etc., it will be more useful to be the watchdog of thought: one will condemn human naïveté and separate the wheat from the chaff.

And, since there is a watchdog, it is less urgent to understand the forger's motives than to identify him. Who is the author of mythology? Who made up this mass of far-fetched and, even worse, indecent legends, from which nursing children derive a false idea of the gods? Who attributed to the gods a conduct unworthy of their holiness? Not too much was known. No one knew the name of the inventor of mythology. However, since a guilty party was necessary, Homer, Hesiod, and other poets served the purpose, ''for it is they, undoubtedly, who gave men these false tales.''[105] They invented some myths, at least. And then, who invented the lies, if not the professionals in mendacious invention? Even when these inventions have a lofty allegorical meaning, they are nonetheless pedagogically dangerous. This is why Homer will be expelled from the city.[106] As we see, Homer is here not the poet we know. He is not the author of the *Iliad* but the supposed creator of all mythology. Plato does not regulate the relationship between the State and *belles-lettres* but that of the State and the collective consciousness. His position is not explained by the Greek idea that every poet creates myths but by this other idea, that all myths were invented by poets.[107]

This rationalism can be countered by a rationalism-and-a-half: can one seriously believe that the poets invented mythology for the pleasure of it? Could imagination be frivolous? It is far too little to say, with Plato, that myths, if well chosen, can be educational. Strabo speculates that every myth has an instructive intention and that the poet did not write the *Odyssey* to entertain but to teach geography.[108] To the rationalist condemnation of the imaginary as false, the apologetic of the imaginary replies that it conforms to a hidden reason. For it is not possible to lie.

Therefore, it is impossible for a myth to be completely mythical. The Greeks could criticize the details of fables, but they could not disregard the fables themselves. The only debate was to decide whether mythology was truthful only in part or in its entirety. The voyages of Odysseus are a course in geography in which everything is veracious, and the legend of Athena born from Zeus's head proves, according to Chrysippus, that technical knowledge is transmitted by speech, which is centered in the head. Myth is truthful, but figuratively so. It is not historical truth mixed with lies; it is a high philosophical teaching that is entirely true, on the condition that, instead of taking it literally, one sees in it an allegory. Two schools exist, then: the criticism of legends by historians and the allegorical interpretation of legends by the majority of philosophers, including the Stoics.[109] From this will emerge the allegorical exegesis of the Bible, destined for fifteen hundred years of triumph.

The assumption behind Stoic allegorism was the same as that of biblical allegorism. The text under consideration was held to be a true authority. Everything that Homer and the other poets said proved it. This is an aspect of Greek thinking about which it is necessary to say a few words. In order to prove something or persuade someone of a truth, a thinker could proceed in at least three ways: develop a line of reasoning reputed to be rigorous, touch the listener's heart by the use of rhetoric, or refer to the authority of Homer or another ancient poet. The Stoics, writes an irritated Galen, are *virtuosi* in matters of logic; but once it is a question of putting this logic into practice on some specific problem, they are worthless and resort to the most hollow mode of argument: they pile up quotations from the poets as evidence.[110]

Rigorous reasoning? A great reader of the *Second Analytics,* Galen knows only syllogistic proofs (he goes so far as to call them geometric).[111] I am not sure whether he has fulfilled his promises in the *De usu partium,* where he demonstrates the finality of each of the organs of the human body by analogy to machines built by men. Claims to rigor and even deduction according to the Aristotelian ideal ordinarily amount to an ethical attitude (one wishes to be serious, one will not say just anything) and to a certain relationship to others. One will make a distinction between demonstration and persuasion and refuse to play on the readers' sensibilities, as rhetoric does. Of course, the rhetorical art also gave speechmakers and orators types of speeches, models of reasoning, and common(or not)-places that needed only to be developed. Nonetheless, the specificity of rhetoric lay in its rejection of a technical, cold appearance in order to persuade by virtue of infectious enthusiasm, insinuating charm, stirring movements, or sometimes a captivating nervous tension. This lay preachers' art was recognized as a perfectly legitimate mode of persuasion—or, rather, the audience was divided between this mode and the preceding one.

But a third mode of persuasion also existed, at least among the founders of Stoicism: to invoke the witness of the poets and, particularly, of Homer. Galen is indignant to see a Chrysippus abandon scientific proof so often and prefer to multiply quotations from Homer,[112] just as rhetoricians seek to impress the judges by calling the greatest possible number of witnesses before the bench. It is in this manner that Chrysippus, wishing to prove that governing reason was lodged in the heart instead of the mind, filled long pages with poetic quotations of this sort: "Achilles resolved in his heart to draw his sword." I do not know whether the true nature of this proof by poetry was recognized among the Stoics, who do not themselves seem to have made a theory of it, but their practice constitutes an implicit theory.

Homer's prestige as a classic, or rather as a focus of national recognition throughout the Greek world, does not count for much here, nor does the prestige of poetry in general;[113] Chrysippus is no Heidegger. Besides Homer, he quotes many other poets and even tragic poets, forgetting that the tragedians put in the mouths of their characters what was demanded by their roles, not by the truth.[114] And, besides poetry, Chrysippus and all the other Stoics quoted myths, the allegorical interpretation of which they had systematically pursued.

For all that, they did not consider that myths and poetry conveyed a revealed wisdom, for they just as often quoted proverbs and etymologies for the same purpose. In their eyes the "etymological" meaning was the "authentic" or "true" meaning (such is the meaning of the word *etymon*). Thus they did not see poetic activity as having a privileged access to the truth, either. What did poetry, myths, etymologies, and proverbs all have in common? Did they serve as a type of proof by general consensus? No, since prose—or, quite simply, any phrase heard from the lips of a passer-by—would then have been equally acceptable as proof. Was it the ancient quality of the evidence? No, since Euripides was also called as a support.

The explanation, I imagine, is that poetry belongs to the same realm as vocabulary, myth, and figures of speech. Far from taking its authority from the poet's genius, poetry, despite the poet's existence, is a sort of authorless speech. It has no locutor; it is what "is said." Thus it cannot lie, since only a locutor would be able to do that. Prose has a speaker, who tells the truth or else lies or is mistaken. But poetry has no more of an author than vocabulary does. It resembles myth, and the profound reason that makes the Greeks say that a poet by definition creates myths is perhaps linked less to the frequency of mythological allusions in poetic works than to the fact that myth and poetry draw their authority from themselves. The truth comes forth from the lips of the poets as naturally as it issues from those of children. They do nothing but reflect things as they are. They express the truth as naturally as springs flow, and they could not reflect what does not exist. It is to be believed that for Chrysippus as much as for Antisthenes, one cannot speak of what is not.[115] Poetry is an involuntary and truthful mirror, and it is because it reflects involuntarily that Chrysippus did not tire of accumulating the evidence of the poets. If in his eyes the poets had been reflective thinkers, who took responsibility for a doctrine, a single quote would have sufficed, as Galen has him note; but they tell the truth as if without thinking of it. Chrysippus, awestruck, does not tire of showing how the basement over which his own philosophy is built continuously allows truth to flow in from all sides.

Since the Stoics are certain beforehand that myth and poetry speak the truth, they have only to put them to torture to reconcile them with this truth. Allegory will furnish this Procrustean bed. The Stoics shrink before nothing. One day Chrysippus was shown a painting in which the salacious*imagination of the *ciceroni* saw Hera inflicting on Zeus an agreeable treatment that cannot be named in decent company. Chrysippus managed to recognize in it an allegory of matter absorbing spermatic Reason in order to engender the cosmos.

For the philosopher, myth was thus an allegory of philosophical truths. For the historians, it was a slight deformation of historical truths. Let it be said in passing that each of these versions is found in Plato—but let us not dwell on a subject that would make the most intrepid of commentators flinch. Sometimes Plato creates his own myths, which are approximations of the Idea, and sometimes, as we have briefly indicated earlier, he encounters some of the Greek historical myths along his way and then subjects them to the same type of criticism that was used by the historians of his time. However, for Plato, philosophical allegory, this half-truth, corresponded to the participation of the sensible in the truth of the Ideas and— notwithstanding this—corresponded also to the impossibility of rigorous knowledge of the sensible. How did the Stoics explain that the poets told the truth by allegory? To hide and reveal the truth in an enigma? Out of some ancient naïveté? And perhaps these thinkers did not consider this question. For the Greeks, the medium disappears behind the message.

Whether as allegories or somewhat altered traditions, myths generally found credence, so that in the middle of the *Metaphysics* an Aristotle, little given to developing facile criticisms, nevertheless judges it opportune to discuss in a tone of scathing irony the legends about ambrosia and nectar, the liquors of immortality.[116] Even those who mistrusted myths did not dare challenge them at their basis; hence their difficulty. This is why they so often seem only to half-believe in their legends or to believe that they believe in them . . . But do partial modalities of belief exist? Were they not rather hesitating between two programs of truth? It was not their faith that was divided, but myth that was half-rotten in their eyes; for it arose from two truths: a criticism of

having a propensity to venery =lustful, lecherous, or inciting lust or sexual wantonness

the unlikely or the unworthy, based on the content, and a rationalism of the imagination, according to which it was impossible for the container to contain nothing and for one to imagine in a void. Therefore, myth always mixed the true and the false. Lies served to adorn the true in order to make it palatable; or else myth told the truth by enigma and allegory; or again, it had come to attach itself to a background of truth.[117] But one could not lie initially. Myth will transmit either some useful teaching, or a physical or theological doctrine hidden under the veil of allegory, or the memory of events of past times.[118] As Plutarch says, truth and myth have the same relationship as the sun to the rainbow, which dissipates light into an iridescent variety.[119]

What interests us in this affair is myth as historical tradition. Since myth as form was never questioned, ancient criticism varied according to its content: to offer a more pious version of the mythical gods or to transform the heroes into historical characters. Legends bring us anecdotes or tales related to the great figures of the heroic times. These are so many sources for history, and what is history? It is the politics of olden times. One will therefore take the myth in a political sense. The Greeks will not be the last to act this way, and Machiavelli will do the same thing again. According to him, Moses was a prince who had to conquer the throne, which presupposes a merit far superior to that possessed by those who only had to take the trouble to inherit one. However, he shares this merit with Cyrus, Romulus, and Theseus, who also conquered power, and, "although one must not speak of Moses, since he only executed the will of God, nevertheless" one will agree that his methods "do not seem very different" from those of other princes. "He who reads the Bible with good sense will see that Moses, to ensure the observation of the Tables of the Law, was constrained to put an infinite number of people to death." Machiavelli had no need for the Bible for this political version of Moses; he had only to read the *Jewish Antiquities* by Flavius Josephus, who subjects Moses to the treatment that Thucydides or Aristotle imposed on Theseus or Minos.[120] And probably with the same secret feeling that one must not foster a childish notion of princes. The great and sublime thing called politics is not made for the naïve. Now, nothing is more naïve than legend. It sees princes with a child's eyes: nothing but love affairs with the gods, extravagant exploits, miracles made to astound old women.

How can the text of the most ancient history be accorded its political seriousness?

Luckily, the thing is possible. For if the unlikely puerilities are obviously false, falsehood, seen from its own standpoint, is nothing but the truth deformed. It is therefore possible to restore the true historical text, and we have seen that Polybius and Aristotle rediscovered the original meaning of Aeolus and the Minotaur. But the most masterful of the correctors was Palaephatus. His principles are very sound: if they have not been educated, men believe everything that is told them; but wise men believe in nothing. The latter are wrong, for everything that has been spoken of has existed (otherwise how would one speak of it?). One merely has to keep strictly to the rule that what is possible is only that which still exists today.[121]

In order to make the transition from myth to history, it will thus be sufficient to correct mistakes that often are simple confusions over words. The centaurs mentioned by the poets are impossible, for, if such hybrid beings had existed, some of them would still be around today. A moment's reflection enables us to see how the legend developed: in order to kill wild bulls, someone invented horseback riding and spearing the quarry with a javelin (*kentō*). Nor did Daedalus make living and moving statues, but he had a more supple and lifelike style than his rivals. Pelops never had winged horses, but he had a ship on which winged horses were painted. Palaephatus, let us note, does not for an instant doubt the historicity of Daedalus, Pelops, and Aeolus (whom he explains in the same manner as Polybius will). He also admits that in these far-off times the gods mingled in human affairs. Athena and Apollo had a hand in the torture of Marsyas, and Apollo actually loved Hyacinth, but it would be childish to believe that this god wrote the name of his lover on the petals of a flower. The truth is that Apollo went no further than giving this flower the name of the beautiful youth.

We see just how far Palaephatus takes rationalist optimism. The text of the truth is not irremediably spoiled, and for a reason. One cannot lie *ex nihilo,* one can only distort the truth. Palaephatus' thinking ceases to be bewildering if we see that it is supported by this idea, dear to the Greeks, as well as by another one: that the problem of rediscovering the original text is defined quite narrowly, for error is multiple and correct meaning unique.

And how does one rediscover this correct meaning? By going against natural inclination. There in fact exists an inclination for distortion among men, who slide over all the obstacles formed by relations between things and their words; they take a word for a thing. one word for another, a painting for reality, a thing for an idea. We see the originality of Palaephatus vis-à-vis the criticism of myths as it had been practiced since Hecataeus: for him, myth has not received foreign additions but has undergone alterations. This is why Palaephatus is the only one to retain the intervention of the gods. He does not measure the mythical past against present reality, in which the gods do not intervene, but considers myth in itself and finds it caricatured by misunderstandings or involuntary puns. Instead of removing the supernatural, he corrects semiological distortions.

Myth is a copy of the past, and it does not so much undergo interpolation as it is altered. Palaephatus does not regard myth as a vehicle for history, transmitting the memory of kings, founders, or masters of the sea. Or at least the only myths that he criticizes are private anecdotes, simple human-interest stories of former times, falsely transformed into the marvelous by semiotic distortion. A myth is born of a pun. Palaephatus reduces the legend of Pandora in this fashion (it matters little how he goes about it) to the story of a rich woman who loved to wear makeup.

These are human-interest stories whose memory has been preserved up to our own time because of the supernatural element that has accrued to them. But it is we who say that, not the Greeks. They never asked themselves why or how the traditions were handed down. They were simply there, and that was enough for the Greeks. They were not for a moment surprised that reflections of the past were among them. They gathered myths everywhere. How did these aerolites come down to them? They do not think about it; perceiving only the message, they do not see the medium. Nor are they surprised that the past has left a memory. It is self-evident that everything has its reflection, just as bodies have shadows. The explanation of myth is the historical reality that it reflects, for a copy is explained by its model. They do not wonder how the reflections could traverse so many centuries, or by what means or for what purpose. Similarly, in the *Cratylus* words are explained by the things that they depict. The role of time is limited to the changes occurring in words, and these alterations hardly merit the name of history. They do not obey phonetic laws; they are aleatory and

stony meteorites

° depending upon uncertain event or contingency as to both profit + loss ; pertaining to or resulting from luck (ie a wager)

inessential. They do not exhibit any regularity and are devoid of interest. Furthermore, one will not posit that myth could have distorted the truth for positive reasons, such as wonder or national emotion. The cause of its alterations is only negative; it resides in a lack of critical spirit. The Greeks never had a science of myth as such, but only a science of the history that myths transmitted. For the mode of transmission does not count. Speech is a simple mirror. By speech, Greeks understood myth, the lexicon (or rather, etymology), poetry, proverbs—in short, everything that "is said" and speaks by itself (since we are only repeating it). Consequently, how could speech speak of nothing? We know what a huge problem the existence of nonbeing was for Greek philosophy up to the time of Plato. This is another symptom of this "discourse" of the mirror that we have just found in the problem of myth. In order to be mistaken, to lie, or to speak about nothing, one must speak of what is not. Thus, what is not must *be,* in order for one to be able to speak of it. But what is a nonbeing that is not nothing? Plato was determined to turn the tide, to kill "our father Parmenides," and, by a stroke as great as that by which Greek mathematicians had just admitted the existence of incommensurable numbers (the famous "irrational" numbers), to admit the existence of nonbeing. We are amazed that it took so great an effort. But if speech is a mirror, the difficulty is understood: how can a mirror reflect what is not there? To reflect what is not comes down to not reflecting; inversely, if the mirror reflects an object, this object exists. Therefore, myth cannot speak of nothing. The conclusion: we are certain in advance that the most naïve of myths will have a truthful basis, and if we ask ourselves, with Palaephatus, about the origin of the errors that one finds in them, we will note that these errors are simple accidents in reproduction. The original was authentic, but, in the process of reflecting it, one word was taken for another, a thing was taken for a word, and so forth.

To reflect nothingness is not to reflect; likewise, to reflect a fog will mean reflecting in a confused way. When the object is cloudy, so is the mirror. Degrees of knowledge will thus be parallel to those of being; all of Platonism is there. The young Aristotle will still be ensnared in the following problem: the principle according to which everything is destructible must therefore itself be destructible; but if this principle perishes, then things cease to perish . . . What is said of things shares the fate of things. A science of what is confused will therefore be a science that is itself confused, a poor speculative knowledge. On the contrary, a science will be noble if the things that it reflects are themselves elevated.

"In the fables of which we were just now speaking," writes Plato, "owing to our ignorance of the truth about antiquity, we liken the false to the true as far as we may. . . ."[122] Plato is not being ironic. Falsehood, we know, is nothing but inexactness, and so we rectify inexact traditions to rediscover what seems to be the truth. In modern terms, we formulate probable historical hypotheses. Beholding their mythical age, the Greeks had two attitudes: a naïveté that wants to believe in order to be charmed, and this sober order of perpetual suspense that we call scientific hypothesis. But they never rediscovered the tranquil assurance with which, once back in the truly historical period, they believed the words of their predecessors, the historians, whom they echo. They express the state of scientific doubt that they maintain before myth as well as they can by saying that the heroic era was too far away, too effaced by time, for them to be able to discern its contours with complete certainty.[123]

6
Restoring Etiological Truth to Myth

To purify myth and make it into an exclusively historical tradition, it will suffice to eliminate everything that has no proven equivalent in our historical era. "I am of an unbelieving disposition with regard to the *mythōdes,* and with good reason; I have never seen anyone who has observed it with his own eyes. One says that another told him about it, the second, that he is of this opinion, and the third forgets everything as soon as a poet speaks."[124] Therefore let us abide by the current realities, which have been properly observed. You tell me that Hercules, mortal that he was, managed to become a god? "I shall certainly call upon you to explain how such a miracle could be accomplished and why it no longer occurs."[125] Present things give us the idea of what is naturally possible. "It is said that the heroes were ten cubits tall. This a charming but misleading and unbelievable myth, if one looks at nature, in which today's individuals are the standard."[126] The reduction of myth to history will require two operations. Palaephatus confined himself to purifying the traditions of what was physically unbelievable; what was historically impossible remained to be eliminated—to wit, the coexistence of gods and mortals. For in our historical age the gods have withdrawn far away from men. Pausanias' troubled evolution, which will furnish most of our examples, unfolds between these two terms.

Nature, say the Epicureans, has, if not laws that would demand that such or such a thing be done, at least pacts or *foedera* that forbid certain things, notably, confusing the boundaries between living species. Thus, metamorphoses would be impossible. It is said that on the banks of the Po a musician became king of the country and that, upon his death, the will of Apollo transformed him into a swan. "I am ready to believe," writes Pausanias, "that a musician became king of the Ligyes, but I cannot believe that a bird grew out of a man."[127] Nor could monsters exist. What is to be done with Cerberus? On the Taenarum was shown the grotto in which Heracles brought the hound of hell to earth. Unfortunately, says Pausanias again, "There is no road that leads underground through the cave, and it is not easy to believe that the gods possess any underground dwelling where the souls collect." It is Hecataeus of Miletus in person who found "a plausible explanation": the "hound" of hell was in fact a giant snake with mortal venom that Heracles killed.[128] The learned did not believe in monsters, hippocentaurs, chimaeras, or Scylla,[129] and Lucretius stated this skepticism in terms of Epicurean physics.[130] And this is why no one any longer believed in the combat between the Giants and the gods: that the gods fought giants who had feet made of serpents is a conception unworthy of their majesty, as well as biologically impossible.[131]

Pausanias is a new Palaephatus. But he is not only that. Homer, who showed the gods mixing with men during the heroic age, tacitly admitted that they had ceased to do so after that time. But since the history of early times resembles that of today, they must not have done so during heroic times, either. A historical myth would be a myth without gods. When gods, men, and beasts mingle on a familiar basis, it was the golden age. But ever since the world became real, the gods hide, and no further communication is possible.[132] "But at the present time," concludes Pausanias, "when sin has grown to such a height and has been spreading over every land and every city, no longer do men turn into gods, except in the flattering words addressed to despots."[133]

Henceforth one could, with Artemidorus, classify mythic traditions according to their cultural dignity.[134] Some traditions are likely, historically as well as naturally, and so they are true. The traditions in which the gods intervene but which remain physically plausible, "are not fundamentally true but are so accepted from the outset by the crowd"—for example, "the tales about Prometheus, Niobe, and the various heroes of tragedy." On the contrary, the legends that run counter to nature, such as "the Gigantomachia, the warriors born from dragons' teeth in Colchis and Thebes, and other similar legends" have "absolutely no basis and are full of nonsense and foolishness." True myths, likely myths, unlikely myths: in history only the first are accepted, but the second are admitted in the general culture; they can furnish tragic subjects and be cited as rhetorical *exempla*,[135] just as modern psychologists and philosophers may refer to examples taken from novels. These *exempla,* say Quintilian and Dion, are, if not believed, at least accepted as arguments. If one dreams of a false but likely myth, Artemidorus advises interpreting the dream in the clear sense; but, if one dreams a foolish dream, the hopes one nurtures will be vain.

The historian owes it to himself to eliminate the gods from the mythical period. Neither Cicero nor Livy believed that Mars was the father of Romulus, and Pausanias does not believe that a nymph was the mother of Orpheus.[136] This is why what we call euhemerism was so pleasing to thinkers of the day. It is impossible to believe in Hercules the god,[137] but it is historically sound to consider Hercules, Bacchus, and the Dioscuri as great men who have, out of human gratitude, been taken for gods or sons of gods.[138] Pausanias, who is a specialist in myth rather than a historian in the strict sense of the word, unblinkingly reports most of the legends he hears, but sometimes, in an outburst, he bans all intervention of the gods from myth. Actaeon, it is said, was torn apart by his dogs by the will of Artemis, but "my own view is that without divine interference the hounds of Actaeon were smitten with madness, and so they were sure to tear to pieces without distinction everybody they chanced to meet."[139] Our mythographer thus goes further than his colleague Palaephatus. Dionysus has no role in Triton's death, or the death of a triton or tritons. It is better to believe another version of the legend, which sees in Dionysus a physical allegory and explains that the fishermen of Tanagra poured wine in the sea to intoxicate a triton that was ravaging the shore and so kill it more easily. For tritons exist, and Pausanias has seen one; in Rome the imperial procurator *a mirabilibus* showed him one, the remains of which were kept in the prince's collections.[140]

The criterion of present things as a measure of everything is a sound principle but delicate to handle. Pausanias doubts many things, but not tritons, and he does not question the birds of Lake Stymphalus either, for they still can be seen in Arabia.[141] Indeed, one must not measure present things against what we know of them.[142] A certain Cleon, from Magnesia ad Sipylum, author of the *Paradoxa,* had noted that people who have never seen anything wrongly deny certain oddities,[143] and Pausanias admits that, when one sacrifices to Eteocles and Polyneices, the flame that rises from the altar consecrated to the enemy brothers miraculously divides into two

73

parts, for this marvel has entered the lists and Pausanias has seen it with his own eyes.[144] The problem, then, lies in knowing the boundaries of reality. Must one believe that Aristomenes, the champion of the Messenians against Sparta, took part in the Battle of Leuctra after his death? If the Chaldaeans, Indians, and Plato are correct in stating that the soul is immortal, it becomes difficult to challenge this myth.[145] And let no one respond that the soul can be immortal and the myth in question be no less of an invention; every myth is presumed to be true, and it is up to the critic to prove its falsity, since truth is more natural than mendacity. Indeed, our philologists repeat, employing a somewhat confused logic, that the text of a manuscript must be taken as true as long as it is not indefensible. . .

The story of reason against myth that we tell here is not an edifying one. For, as we will see, reason has not won (the problem of myth was forgotten rather than resolved); it was not fighting for a good cause (the principle of "current things" was the bastion of all prejudices—in its name Epicurus and Saint Augustine denied the existence of the Antipodes); and, finally, it was not reason that was engaged in the battle, but only a program of truth whose presuppositions are so strange that they elude us or astound us when we do grasp them. One never possesses a complete vision of truth, falsehood, myth, or superstition, or evidence of them, an *index sui*. Thucydides believed in oracles,[146] Aristotle, in dream divination; Pausanias obeyed his dreams.[147]

Once the inexactitudes of tradition have been corrected, authentic facts are obtained. Mythological literature, whether oral or written—with its innumerable authors, known or unknown, and its multiple variants—will henceforth compete with everyday reality. It will have to have the chronological, prosopographical, and biographical coherence of history. Therefore, if a tomb belonging to Oedipus existed in Athens, it would be necessary to adjust this information with the rest: "Within the precincts is a monument to Oedipus, whose bones, after diligent inquiry, I found were brought from Thebes. The account of the death of Oedipus in the drama of Sophocles I am prevented from believing by Homer," who said that Oedipus had died and was buried at Thebes.[148]

Mythical time had neither depth nor breadth.[149] One might as well wonder whether the adventures of Tom Thumb took place before or after Cinderella's ball. Nevertheless, the heroes, those noble personages, had a genealogical tree. It would also occur that a hero would hear a prediction that the misfortunes of his family would come to an end five or ten generations after him.[150] Thus, at an early date mythographers could establish a chronology of mythical generations. One was no longer reduced to saying, "Once upon a time there was a king and a nymph"; one could prevail over those who questioned legends because they contained no chronology,[151] and with the aid of synchronisms,[152] one could distinguish the false legends from the true. Already Isocrates could avenge Busiris of a rhetorician's calumnies by proving that Busiris predated by six centuries that Heracles who, it was claimed, had punished him for certain crimes.[153] Prosopography became no less systematic. Homonymies were discussed and dismissed (Pausanias established that the Telamon whose tomb could be seen at Pheneüs is not the father of Ajax but an obscure homonym).[154] Certain events, it was determined, must have happened more than once. Since the oldest recorded Olympic victory dated back to 776 B.C., it had been concluded that this date was also that of the founding of the contest. But, since it was known that Apollo had triumphed over Hermes and Ares at Olympia, it had to be imagined that a first Olympic contest had been instituted in very ancient times, had fallen into disuse, and had then been revived in 776. Such an invention had the earmarks of a historian in the style of Diodorus or a philologist for whom texts are the true reality. Strabo and Pausanias, for their part, do not believe it for an instant.[155] Their conception of the gods is less naïve.

Nevertheless, this obsession with rigorous chronology is significant. As it does to this day, the law of the historical genre required that events are narrated by giving their date—to the very day, if possible. What is the reason for this often useless precision? Because chronology is the eye of history, and it enables one to control or refute hypotheses? It is true that chronology makes this possible, but this is not why so much value is attached to it. Chronology, like geography and prosopography, is first of all a self-sufficient program of truth in which time and space are known when what they contain can be put into place—men, events, and localities. It is the most artless of the conceptions of history. When one knows how to appreciate a painting one is an esthete; but if one can date it, one is an art historian and knows what comprises the past of painting. So the Greeks extracted a historical chronology from heroic genealogies, and

75

mythical time, analogous to our own, preceded it until the fateful date of about 1200 B.C., the time of the Trojan War and the moment when purely human history begins.[156]

What was it necessary to know in order to be familiar with the history of the heroic ages? Genealogies. The foundation of Patrae, to take this example from among a hundred others, was the work of Patreus, the son of Preugenes and the grandson of Agenor, and it was he who gave his name to the city. This Agenor had for a father Areus, the son of Ampys, himself the son of Pelias, the son of Aeginetes, the son of Dereites, the son of Harpalus, the son of Amyclas, the son of Lacedaemon.[157] Complete knowledge of the past was reduced to acquiring a complete list of kings or archetypes, without omitting the blood ties that bind them, either. Then one possessed the thread of the times. Poets and local historians wove this thread everywhere. Myth, this authorless "it is said" that is confused with the truth, was reinterpreted as a historical or cultural memory which, starting with the eyewitnesses, would be handed down from generation to generation. If one wished to know the origins of a city, one had to ask the local inhabitants. The grammarian Apion, who wanted to know what game Penelope's suitors were playing with their counters while seated before the gate of the *megaron,* asked the question of an inhabitant of Ithaca.[158] Pausanias acted no differently. He visited Greece city by city, and in every town he spoke with those leading citizens who were interested in local origins and who often possessed a copy of a work by a little-known historian. Together these scholars and these books constitute what Pausanias calls the "exegetes of antiquities," who were wrongly seen as *ciceroni* or sacristans.[159] Most often Pausanias does not give us their names. An ancient historian, as we know, does not use footnotes.

But why was the thread of time genealogical? Because myths recount the biographies of heroes, kings, and archetypes. This old oral literature spoke only of origins, foundations, and warlike exploits, of family dramas with princely actors. We have seen that archetypes, such as Hellen or Pelasgus, were considered ancient kings the moment that the myth was interpreted as historical tradition. The history of the city was the history of its royal family. The heroes, too, were princely personalities. It was concluded from this that "everywhere in Greece in ancient times, kingship and not democracy was the established form of government."[160] The touching mythical literature that depicted the family dramas was offered in the guise of serious history. The archaic history of the Achaeans[161] was no less filled with palace revolts than that of the Seleucids or the Lagids. In the hands of Pausanias the war of the Seven against Thebes becomes a kind of Peloponnesian War, and "the most memorable of all those that Greeks waged against Greeks in what is called the heroic period," as our writer says, openly imitating Thucydides.[162] Argos and Thebes each had allied cities throughout Hellas. The conflict spanned several periods and included sieges, open warfare, and decisive battles.

In the course of the Hellenistic and Roman periods there thus grew up in this fashion the enormous local historiography, masterfully studied by the great Louis Robert, which accorded each city its origins and ancestors—details that enabled politicians to invoke a legendary kinship between cities in order to found an alliance or make a demand for services, whether great or small. These bonds were often surprising, as between Lanuvium and Centuripes, Sparta and Jerusalem, Rome and Troy.[163] It could be called a forger's historiography, in which everything is invented on the basis of minuscule signs or taken from the author's imagination. Until an extremely recent period, the modern era had a dynastic or regional historiography that was no less imaginary.[164]

We should not seek to find any metaphysical torment in this ideology of origins. It was not a misdirected search for the resonance that a foundation story could provide. Etiology simply spoke from a need for political identity.

Indeed, what was strange in this local historiography was that it was reduced to a question of origins. It did not tell of the life of the city, its collective memories or great moments. It was enough to know when and how the city had been founded. Once created, the city had only to live its life, which could be presumed to be comparable to what city life can be and which would be what it could be. It was not important. Once the historian had narrated its foundation, the city was fixed in space and time; it had its identity card.

This fixing of identities was a familiar mode of knowledge among the Ancients. Certain epitaphs identify the deceased in this way, and Virgil imitates them in two beautiful lines on the death of the warrior Eolus: "There your mortal limits lay: a high abode at the foot of Ida, in Lyrnesse, a high abode, and, in the Laurentine land, a tomb." And such will be Virgil's own epitaph: "Mantua gave me light, Calabria took it away from me.'' Similarly, I read the following in the *Petit Larousse* of 1908: "Zichy (Eugène de), Hungarian politician and explorer, born in Zichyfalva in 1837; Zeigler (Claude), French painter, born in London (1804–1856)."

Thus, thanks to etiology, even the most obscure of Greek cities has its personality. It will be a moral person, a full member in the society of cities. It will be comparable to a man who is fully a man, a freeborn man. Such cities "from birth are notable and did not begin as slaves," writes Menander the Rhetorician in the treatise he devoted to set speeches for orators to use to praise a city before its inhabitants.[165]

7
Myth and Rhetorical Truth

To say that, as a consequence, myth became a political ideology is not false, but it does not help us very much. A detail leads us beyond these generalities: the Greeks often seem not to believe very much in their political myths and were the first to laugh at them when they flaunted them on ceremonial occasions. Their use of etiology was formal; in fact, myth had become rhetorical truth. One imagines, then, that what they felt was less disbelief, strictly speaking, than a feeling of conventionality or derision in response to the fixed character of this mythology. Hence, a special modality of belief: the content of set speeches was perceived not as true or, moreover, as false, but as verbal. The obligations of this "stock language" devolve not to the side of political power but to an institution peculiar to the period: rhetoric. Nevertheless, interested parties were not against it, for they could distinguish between the letter and the good intention: although it was not true, it was well said.

The Greeks had long been kindly disposed toward the *bene trovato*, which confirms an idea of the young Nietzsche: a lie does not exist if the liar has no motive for lying.[166] One cannot be lying when speaking more highly of values than one strictly should. The Homeric Hymn to Hermes offers an amusing illustration of this pious zeal. According to the poet, the god Hermes, the young prodigy full of malicious impulses, had hardly left his mother's womb when he invented the art of singing. The first composition of this privileged witness consisted in telling of the loves of his father and mother. The crowd of pilgrims who heard this hymn recited for the first time must have felt like public accessories and applauded wholeheartedly. No one was taken in by the clever tale, but they expected no less of Hermes and were grateful to the poet for inventing this legend.

For these pilgrims were good people; they had respect for values.

Serious persons of responsible character will indeed make the noble decision concerning the following case: can one without pedantry condemn someone who zealously embraces the good cause—that of the Good, which is also that of the True—for reasons that contain no literal truth? Is it not better to ignore this purely verbal inaccuracy? When true values are evident, a similar indifference to veracity defines a whole series of historically diversified conducts. Throughout Greece these verbal behaviors, in which language informs less than it fulfills a function, occur in the area of international relations. In internal politics they were represented in a literary genre: the panegyric of the city, pronounced before its citizens.

In 480 B.C., the day after their triumph over the Persians at Salamis, the Greeks convened in a congress. The definitive victory was in sight, and already Athens, which had saved all of Hellas from the barbarians, appeared as the hegemonical city. It had the power and possessed the language for it. When another city decided to oppose to this new primacy its own traditional privileges, the Athenians replied that their own rights were no less ancient. For Athens had been victorious in the times of the Heraclidae, the wars recounted in the *Thebaïd,* and the invasion of the Amazons.[167] Everyone understood what the speechifying meant, and Athens won its case. The mythical titles had served to designate relations of force by justifying them, which dispensed the Athenians from having to name them. Is this an ideological cover? The relationship is not one of superposition, as is that between a blanket and what lies beneath; it is the relationship between the paper money of words and the gold depositary of power. Was it a threat couched in praise? It was more than that. By referring to lofty reasons instead of making a show of force, one encourages the other to submit willingly and for honorable reasons, which saves face. Ideology is not a mere echo of reality; it works like a coin inserted in a machine. In international society, mythical titles to glory, as well as legendary kinship among peoples, served as ceremonial salutes.[168] Each city would state its legendary origins to its partners, who took care not to be skeptical. It was a way of affirming oneself as a person. The society of cities thus was composed of noble persons who had their bonds of kinship. Accepting these fictions as articles of faith signaled recognition of the rules of the international life of civilized cities.

It is curious that this affirmation of the personality of each city, like the creation of individuality by fixing it in space and time, played an equally great role in internal politics. Indeed, the pleasure that citizens took in hearing an orator pronounce the panegyric of their city cannot be believed. These speeches of praise were a fashion that lasted for a millennium, up to the end of Antiquity. People spoke of mythical origins and of kinship among the cities of Greece as often as the people who frequented the salons of the faubourg Saint-Germain talked genealogy, and for the same reasons.[169] Whether he was a native or came from another city, the orator celebrated the origins of the city, and this was not the least of the praises he would lavish. The citizens took the greatest pleasure in hearing him. "When I hear praised," Socrates says ironically, "those who have just died in battle and, with them, our ancestors, our city, and ourselves, I feel more noble and great; each of the other listeners feels the same on his part, so that the entire civic body comes out of it exalted, and it takes me three days to get over this emotion."[170]

In the absurdities, discomforts, and small ironies of daily life, more serious processes are brought into awareness. All cities, large or small, had their origin, and one can praise all of them. Manuals of rhetoric furnish recipes for discovering some merit in no matter what little hole-in-the-wall. Moreover, these panegyrics aimed less at exalting one city above all others than at recognizing its dignity as a person. And these words of praise were addressed less to the group than to the individuals within it. In the panegyrics spoken before the assembled city, it was not the group that worshiped itself, as was the case in Nuremberg. The praises of the city made each citizen feel, not that he was carried by a collective force, but rather that, in addition to his other merits, he had another personal dignity, the quality of citizen. The glorification of the group was the glorification of individuals, as if one had praised nobility in front of a group of nobles. It was not patriotic pride; the individual was proud, not to belong to that city rather than another one, but to be a citizen instead of not being one. For citizenship was not felt to be a universal trait, a sort of baseline of individuality, as it is with us, where one is French or German because one cannot not be something. It did not matter that everyone might belong to a city; that made one no less proud of being a citizen. To explain why, it would be necessary to search the hidden part of the iceberg of ancient politics. Let us say only that the city was not a "population." It was not the human fauna that mere chance of birth brought together within a particular territorial limit. Each city felt itself to be a sort of constituted body, in the manner of a corporation of the French Old Regime or the Order of Notaries or Physicians. A strange privilege, in this Hellas or Roman Empire, where every free man, or nearly, is the citizen of some city. It can be understood that the contradiction of universal privilege would have given rise to some uneasiness in the subconscious of the interested parties. This vague torment gave rise to a vivid sense of pleasure when a panegyric was heard in which one of the two terms of the contradiction was exalted to the exclusion of the other.

For we are capable of reacting affectively to contradictions of which we are not clearly aware. Without knowing the reason, on such occasions we experience that uneasy reaction called the sense of the ridiculous. The Greeks were the first to make fun of their taste for civic panegyrics: "You are, O Athenians, a people of dupes. When the deputies of the subject towns wished to fool you, they began by calling you brilliant Athens, and, upon hearing that, you sat down on your behinds." In the work of another comic poet, a seller of girls who has brought suit against one of his clients recalls to the jury that their justice must show itself worthy of the founders of their city, Heracles and Asclepius.[171] Uneasiness and doubt can arise from a dysfunction as well. In the diplomatic field, invocations of great ancestors took the place of solid reasons when more substantial interests were lacking. They became ridiculous formalities when these interests existed and the occasion demanded that one speak of business.[172]

Another source of skepticism was the presence of rhetoric constituted as a self-conscious technique. People had learned the arts of persuasion or how to turn a phrase in school and were not taken in by them.[173] Sometimes they carried bad faith to the point of didacticism. In his *Panegyric of Athens,* Isocrates wants the reader to seek proofs of Athenian grandeur and generosity in the time "well before the Trojan War," and he adds that, "even though the account of these proofs is *mythōdes,* it is no less proper to give it."[174] How can this orator be so clumsy as to contradict his own assertions? Because he is also a teacher of rhetoric, and so he comments on each of his oratorical effects for his readers' instruction.

One more source was the nonprofessional quality of the historian's activity. We saw earlier that the fine name of historian was borne equally by authors, such as Diodorus, who intended above all to divert their readers or foster in them their own pious convictions, and by "serious," indeed "pragmatic" historians, who meant to leave edifying lessons for the politicians. At least this was what they said. In fact, they particularly intended to leave future politicians some interesting, if not instructive, stories that spotlighted their colleagues in the political corporation—for the shoemaker likes to hear about shoemakers. Such is the case for the *ktēma es aei** of Thucydides and his history lessons. Thus, there were serious history books, and there were also many of them that were not so serious; but the most important thing is that no external sign differentiated the first from the second. The public was reduced to judging them on an individual basis. As we see, nonprofessionalization had harmful effects. Let us hasten to add that current academic professionalization also has such effects, as well as others no less perverse, although academic sociologists, not surprisingly, seem to be less aware of them. Nevertheless, the blending of best and worst misled minds, ruined the readers' moral nature, and fostered a sly skepticism. It thus was necessary for the historians of the day to tactfully manage all the inclinations of a rather mixed audience. When Livy or Cicero in *De re publica* write that Rome is enough of a big city for people to respect the tales with which she adorned her origins, they are not bluffing their readers with ideological stories—quite the contrary. As good reporter-historians, they disdainfully allow each of their readers to choose his preferred version of the facts. Nonetheless, they reveal that on their part they do not believe a word of these tales.

We see how far ancient artlessness was removed from ideological dictatorship or edifying pretenses. The function created its organ, the "stock languages" of etiology or rhetoric, but no political or religious authority contributed its weight. Compared to the Christian or Marxist centuries, Antiquity often has a Voltairean air. Two soothsayers cannot meet without smirking at each other, writes Cicero. I feel I am becoming a god, said a dying emperor.

This poses a general problem. Like the Dorzé, who imagine both that the leopard fasts and that one must be on guard against him every

---

*Literally, "a possession for all time." Rex Warner, in the Penguin edition, translates: "My work is not a piece of writing designed to meet the taste of an immediate public, but was done to last for ever" (Thuc. 1.22). In the first part of this sentence, Thucydides is referring, invidiously, to Herodotus.

day, the Greeks believe and do not believe in their myths. They believe in them, but they use them and cease believing at the point where their interest in believing ends. It should be added in their defense that their bad faith resided in their belief rather than in their ulterior motives. Myth was nothing more than a superstition of the half-literate, which the learned called into question. The coexistence of contradictory truths in the same mind is nonetheless a universal fact. Lévi-Strauss's sorcerer believes in his magic and cynically manipulates it. According to Bergson, the magician resorts to magic only when no sure technical recipes exist. The Greeks question the Pythia and know that sometimes this prophetess makes propaganda for Persia or Macedonia; the Romans fix their state religion for political purposes by throwing sacred fowl into the water if these do not furnish the necessary predictions; and all peoples give their oracles—or their statistical data—a nudge to confirm what they wish to believe. Heaven helps those who help themselves; Paradise, but the later the better. How could one not be tempted to speak of ideology here?

If we are able to believe in contradictory things, it is probably because in some cases the knowledge we have of an object is distorted by our interests. For objects set in the sphere of reality exist naturally, and a natural light of the mind is reflected off them and back to us. Sometimes the light comes to us directly, at others it is influenced by imagination—or passion, as they said in the seventeenth century—or by authority, or interest, as we say today. And so the same object gives off two reflections, and the second is distorted. Ideology is a *tertium quid* next to the truth and to the inevitable and haphazard breakdowns of truth known as errors. Ideology is a constant and directed error. What lends plausibility to this scheme is that it recalls the old idea of temptation and corruption; interest and money can twist the most righteous conscience.

The notion of ideology is a laudable and unsuccessful attempt to guard against the legend of the idea of a disinterested knowledge, at the limits of which there would exist a natural understanding, an autonomous faculty, different from the interests of practical life. Unfortunately, this attempt ends in a rough compromise: ideology blends two irreconcilable conceptions of knowledge, reflection and operation. Hardly striking at first sight; but if one thinks about it for a moment, this contradiction is redhibitory: knowledge cannot be correct and biased at the same time. If forces such as class interest or power sway it when it is false, then the same forces also obtain when it speaks the truth. Knowledge is the product of these forces, not the reflection of its object.

It would be better to admit that no knowledge is disinterested and that truths and interests are two different terms for the same thing; for practice thinks what it does. It was desirable to make a distinction between truth and interest only in order to explain the limitations of the former; it was thought that the truth was bounded by the influence of interests. This is to forget that interests themselves are limited (in every age they fall within historical limits; they are arbitrary in their fierce interestedness) and that they have the same boundaries as the corresponding truths. They are inscribed within the horizons that the accidents of history assign to different programs.

If this were not the case, it would seem paradoxical that interests can be the victims of their own ideology. If one were to forget that practices and interests are limited and *rare,* one would take Athenian and Hitlerian imperialism for two examples of an eternal Imperialism, and then Hitlerian racism would be nothing more than an ideological blanket—a motley one, to be sure, but what does that matter? Since the only function of racism is to justify totalitarianism or fascism, the Hitlerian version would be only a superstition or a sham. Then one would note with astonishment that Hitler, because of his racism, sometimes compromised the success of his totalitarian imperialism. The truth is less complicated. Hitler confined himself to putting his racist ideas, which were what interested him, into practice. Jackel and Trevor-Roper have shown that his true war aim was the extermination of the Jews and the extension of Germanic colonization throughout the Slavic states. For him Russians, Jews, and Bolsheviks amounted to the same thing, and he did not think that his persecution of the first two would compromise his victory over the latter . . . Just because one is "interested" does not mean that one is rational; even class interests are the products of chance.

Since interests and truths do not arise from "reality" or a powerful infrastructure but are jointly limited by the programs of chance, it would be giving them too much credit to think that the eventual contradiction between them is disturbing. Contradictory truths do not reside in the same mind—only different programs, each of which encloses different truths and interests, even if these truths have the same name. I know a doctor who is a passionate homeopath but who nonetheless has the wisdom to prescribe antibiotics in serious cases; he reserves homeopathy for mild or hopeless situations. His good faith is whole, I attest to it. On the one hand, he wants to take pleasure in unorthodox medicines, and, on the other, he is of the opinion that the interest of both doctor and patient is that the patient recovers. These two programs neither contradict each other nor have anything in common, and the apparent contradiction emerges only by taking the corresponding truths literally, which demand that one be a homeopath or not. But truths are not sprinkled like stars on the celestial sphere; they are the point of light that appears at the end of the telescope of a program, and so two different truths obviously correspond to two different programs, even if they go by the same name.

This is not without interest in the history of beliefs. We do not suffer when our mind, apparently contradicting itself, secretly changes programs of truth and interest, as it unceasingly does. This is not ideology; it is our most habitual way of being. A Roman who manipulates the state religions according to his political ends can be of as good faith as my friend the homeopath. If he is acting in bad faith, it will be because he does not believe in one of his two programs while he is using it; it will not be because he believes in two contradictory truths. Besides, bad faith is not always found where we think it is. Our Roman could be sincerely pious. If he affects a religious scruple that he scarcely believes in in order to call off an election in which the people are likely to make a poor choice, this does not prove that he does not believe in his gods; it proves only that he does not believe in the state religion and holds it to be a useful imposture invented by men. Even more likely, he will think that all the values must be defended together, religion or fatherland, and that a reason is never a bad one when it supports a good cause.

Our daily life is composed of a great number of different programs, and the impression of quotidian mediocrity is precisely the result of this plurality, which in some states of neurotic scrupulosity is sensed as hypocrisy. We move endlessly from one program to another the way we change channels on the radio, but we do it without realizing it. Religion is only one of these programs, and it rarely acts within the others.

As Paul Pruyser says in his *Dynamic Psychology of Religion*, religion occupies only the slightest part of a religious man's thoughts during the day, but the same could be said of a sports fan, militant, or poet. It occupies a narrow band, but it does so genuinely and intensely. The author of these lines has long felt uneasy with historians of religion. They sometimes seemed to him not only to make their object into a monolith, when the mind in fact is not a stone, but to accord religion an actual predominance over other practices that befits the importance it theoretically has. Daily life contradicts these noble illusions. Religion, politics, and poetry may well be the most important things in this world or any other; nevertheless, in practice they occupy only a narrow band of our existence, and they tolerate contradiction all the more easily since it generally passes unnoticed. This does not mean that these beliefs are any less sincere and intense. The metaphysical importance or individual sincerity of a truth is not measured by its wavelength. In any case, we speak of truths in the plural and believe that the history of religions has something to gain from this.

One feels more at ease studying beliefs, religious or otherwise, when one understands that truth is plural and analogical. This analogy among the true makes the heterogeneity of the programs go unsuspected. We continue to be within the true when we unwittingly change wavelengths. Our sincerity is complete when we forget the imperatives and usages of the truth of five minutes ago in order to adopt those of the new one.

The different truths are all true in our eyes, but we do not think about them with the same part of our head. In a passage in *Das Heilige,* Rudolf Otto analyzes the fear of ghosts. To be exact, if we thought about ghosts with the same mind that makes us think about physical facts, we would not be afraid of them, or at least not in the same way. We would be afraid as we would be of a revolver or of a vicious dog, while the fear of ghosts is the fear of the intrusion of a different world. For my part, I hold ghosts to be simple fictions but perceive their truth nonetheless. I am almost neurotically afraid of them, and the months I spent sorting through the papers of a dead friend were an extended nightmare. At the very moment I type these pages I feel the hairs stand up on the back of my neck. Nothing would reassure me more than to learn that ghosts "really" exist. Then they would be a phenomenon like any other, which could be studied with the right instruments, a camera or a Geiger counter. This is why science fiction, far from frightening me, delightfully reassures me.

Is this phenomenology? No, it is history, and doubly so. Husserl, in *Erfahrung und Urteil,* has given us a suggestive description of what he calls the world of the imaginary. The time and space of stories are not those of what he calls the world of real experience, and there individuation remains incomplete. Zeus is only a figure from a tale, without true civic standing, and it would be absurd to wonder if he seduced Danaë before or after he ravished Leda.

Except that Husserl, in a very classic manner, is of the mind that a transhistorical ground of truth exists. First of all, it would be rather unhistorical to distinguish between experience and a world of the imaginary in which the truth would be not only different but lesser; second, the number and structure of experiential or imaginary worlds are not an anthropological constant but vary throughout history. The only constant of truth lies in its claim to truth, and this claim is only a formal one. The content of norms it embodies depends on the society or, to put it differently: in the same society there are several truths, which, despite their differences, are each as true as the other. What does "imaginary" mean? What is imaginary is the reality of others, just as, according to a phrase of Raymond Aron, ideologies are the ideas of others. "Imaginary"—unlike "image"—is not a psychologist's or anthropologist's term but expresses a dogmatic judgment concerning certain beliefs of another. If our intent is not to dogmatize on the existence of God or the gods, we must confine ourselves to stating that the Greeks held their gods to be true, although these gods existed for them in a space-time that was secretly different from the one in which their believers lived. This belief of the Greeks does not oblige us to believe in their gods, but it says a great deal regarding what the truth is for men.

Sartre used to say that the imaginary is an *analogon* of the real. One could say that the imaginary is the name we give to certain truths and that all truths are analogous. These different worlds of truth are historical artifacts, not psychic constants. Alfred Schutz tried to draw up a philosophical list of these different worlds, and in his *Collected Papers* one can read his studies, the titles of which are revealing: "On Multiple Realities" and "Don Quixote and the Problem of Reality." When a historian reads them, he feels slightly disappointed. The multiple realities that Schutz discovers in the psyche are the ones that find credence in our time, but they are a bit faded and somewhat vague, which gives them an aura of eternity. This phenomenology is, unwittingly, in fact contemporary history, and one would search there in vain for the Greek beliefs regarding myth.

Schutz nonetheless has the merit of articulating the plurality of our worlds, which historians of religions sometimes fail to recognize. Let us examine another one of these stock languages that served as ideology among the Ancients: the divinization of the sovereign. The Egyptians took their pharaoh for a god, the Greco-Romans divinized their emperors alive or dead, and we recall that Pausanias saw nothing but "vain flattery" in these apotheoses. Did people really believe in them? One fact shows just where our duplicity with ourselves leads: although the emperors were gods, and although archeologists have found tens of thousands of ex-votos offered to different deities for healing, safe returns, etc., not one ex-voto offered to an emperor-god exists. When the faithful needed a true god, they did not turn to the emperor. And yet there are no less striking proofs that the same faithful considered the sovereign to be more than human, a kind of magus or thaumaturge.

Struggling to determine "the" true thought of these people is pointless, and it is equally unproductive to attempt to resolve these contradictory thoughts by attributing one to popular religion and the other to the beliefs of the privileged social classes. The faithful did not consider their all-powerful master to be an ordinary man, and the official hyperbole that made of this mortal a god was true in spirit. It corresponded to their filial devotion. Swept on by the linguistic tide, they experienced this feeling of dependence all the more strongly. However, the absence of votive offerings proves that they did not take the hyperbole literally. They also knew that their sublime master was at the same time a poor man, in the same way that at Versailles they made a cult of the Grand Monarch and gossiped about his slightest movements. G. Posener has shown that in the popular tales of ancient Egypt the pharaoh is nothing more than a banal and sometimes ridiculous potentate. Nevertheless, in this same Egypt, intellectuals, theologians, and others elaborated a pharaonic theology in which the pharaoh is not divinized by simple hyperbole or metonymical shifting. This doctrine was "an intellectual discovery, the fruit of metaphysical and theological arguments," writes François Daumas, who, by a contradictory and ingenious expression, endows it with linguistic reality. Why not? The constitutional texts of the nineteenth and twentieth centuries, the Declaration of the Rights of Man, and official

Marxism, are no less real and no less linguistic in nature. In Greece and Rome, on the other hand, the divinity of the emperors was never made the object of an official doctrine, and the skepticism of Pausanias was the rule among the intellectuals and among the emperors themselves, who sometimes were the first to laugh at their divinity.

All of this is truly history, since myths, apotheoses, and Declarations of Rights, imaginary or not, were nonetheless historical forces, and since an imaginary world, where the gods can be mortals and are male or female, can be dated: it precedes Christianity. It is history for another reason as well: these truths are only the clothing of forces; they are practices, not the light that guides them. When men depend on an all-powerful man, they experience him as a man and see him from a valet's perspective as a mere mortal; but they also experience him as their master and therefore also see him as a god. The plurality of truths, an affront to logic, is the normal consequence of the plurality of forces. The thinking reed is humbly proud to oppose his weak and pure truth to brute forces, yet all the while this truth is one of these forces. Thought belongs to the infinitely pluralized monism of the will to power. All types of forces enter into play: political power, professional authority in knowledge, socialization, and training. And because thought is a force, it is not separated from practice the way the soul is from the body. It is a part of it. Marx spoke of ideology to emphasize that thought was action and not pure understanding; but as a materialist of the old school he attached the soul to the body instead of not distinguishing the one from the other and handling practice as a unit. This has forced historians to perform dialectic exercises (the soul reacts on the body) to straighten out the muddle.

Truth is Balkanized by forces and blocked by forces. Worship and love of the sovereign reflect the efforts of the subjugated to gain the upper hand: "Since I love him, therefore he must wish me no harm." (A German friend told me that his father had voted for Hitler to reassure himself; since I vote for him, Jew that I am, it is because in his heart he believes as I do.) And, if the emperor demanded or, more often, allowed himself to be worshiped, this served as "threatening information." Since he can be worshiped, let no one think to contest his authority. The Egyptian theologians who elaborated a whole ideology of the king-god must indeed have had some interest in doing so, even if it were only to provide themselves with an uplifting novel. Under France's Old Regime, people believed and wanted to believe in the king's kindness and that the entire problem was the fault of his ministers. If this were not the case, all was lost, since one could not hope to expel the king the way one could remove a mere minister. As we see, causality is always at work, even among those who supposedly undergo its effects. The master does not inculcate an ideology in the slave; he has only to show that he is more powerful. The slave will do what he can to react, even creating an imaginary truth for himself. The slave undertakes what Léon Festinger—a psychologist with an innate shrewdness, whose insights are instructive—calls a reduction of dissonance.

Psychology indeed, for often the contradictions between behaviors can be observed and so betray the movement of underlying forces. Bad conscience and bad faith emerge, or Phariseeism. Daily life is full of them, and a whole anecdotal psychology will enable us to finish up more quickly in a minor mode. Since forces are the truth of truths, we know only what we are allowed to know. We are genuinely ignorant of what we do not have the right to learn. ''Never confess,'' Proust advised the author of *Corydon;* in this way no one will see what is staring him in the face, for the justice of the *salon* admits only confessions and reproves the one who sets himself up as the inquisitor of his peers. Similarly, betrayed husbands are blind because, without a hint of proof, they have no right to suspect their wives. Their only option is ignorance, unless a fact comes to light right before their eyes. But what they do not know is far too much. You can hear their silence.

In Béroul's *Tristan* there is an episode that sets one to speculating. Yseut has left King Marc and fled with Tristan into the forest. After three years have passed, one morning the lovers awake feeling nothing for each other. The love potion, whose effects for Béroul are not eternal, has exhausted its potency. Tristan decides that the wisest course is for Yseut to return to her husband. So he brings her back to Marc, challenging to combat anyone who would claim that he had ever touched Yseut. No one took up the glove, and the queen's innocence was incontestable. What did Béroul or his readers think of this? Nothing here can replace the text and its unfathomable artlessness.

Béroul indeed feels that, as a jealous lover, Marc knew everything but that, as husband and king, he had no right to know. For Marc and for Béroul this conflict takes place on a conscious level, or rather at a level situated just beneath it, where we know full well what it is we must not discover. Betrayed husbands and blind parents see what they must not see from a long way off, and the furious and anguished tone of voice with which they instantly retort leaves no doubt concerning their unwitting lucidity. Between this blindness and bad faith and the verbiage of formal salutations, all psychological degrees are conceivable. The same was true among the Greeks in matters of myth, beginning with Isocrates. Plato betrays an uneasy state of mind when he says in book 7 of the *Laws* that he has two reasons for believing that women are capable of being good soldiers. "On the one hand, I have faith in a myth that is told," that of the Amazons, "and, on the other, I know [for that is the word] that, in our day," the women of the tribe of the Sauromatians practice archery. Yet psychological anecdotes are one thing, and the constitutive imagination is another. Despite his bad conscience, or rather because of it, Plato does not reject myths but seeks their undisputed kernel of truth, since such was the program of which he, along with all his contemporaries, was prisoner.

Nonetheless, we know (or believe—it is the same thing) only what we have the right to know. Lucidity remains the captive of this relationship of force, which easily passes itself off as superior ability. The result can be observed in a certain number of exemplary cases. We have already seen that it is important to *know that opinions are divided,* and this results in the Balkanization of each mind. Unless one cultivates disrespect as a heuristic method, one does not simply dismiss out loud what many believe, and, by the same token, one does not condemn it mentally, either. One believes in it a bit oneself. It is no less important to *know what can be known.* Raymond Ruyer wrote somewhere that, to make the atomic bomb, the Russians did not absolutely have to spy on the Americans; they only needed to know that it was possible to make such a bomb, which they learned as soon as they heard that the Americans had made one. Herein lies the entire superiority of cultural "inheritors." We can see it by contrast in the case of the self-taught. What is crucial for them is not that they hear about good books but that these are indicated to them by people who, like themselves, are self-taught. Then they will imagine that it is possible to understand these books because their peers have understood them. An inheritor is someone who knows that there is no arcane knowledge; he assumes that he is capable of doing as much as his parents succeeded in doing, and, if hidden knowledge were involved, his parents had access to it. For it is of prime importance to *know that others know* or, on the contrary, to know that there is nothing more to know and that, beyond the small field of knowledge that one possesses, there does not exist a danger zone where only others, who are more competent, may venture. If one believes that arcane domains accessible only to others exist, research and invention are paralyzed. One does not dare take a step all alone.

In a rosy vision of things, the social distribution of knowledge (everyone does not know everything, and each one benefits from the competence of others) results in effects that are as neutral and beneficial as the exchange of goods in the economists' perfect market. What could be more innocent or more disinterested than knowledge of the truth? It is the opposite of brutal relationships. It is true that there is competence and competence. In book 4 of the *Laws,* this time Plato sets in opposition the servile knowledge of the doctor's slave, who applies, without understanding them, the procedures his master has taught him, and the true competence of the free man, the doctor, who knows the why of these procedures and who, having pursued liberal studies, ''knows according to nature.'' It is indeed true that the long training of our engineers and doctors enables them to understand the reasons for the techniques they apply and, consequently, perhaps to invent new ones. It is no less true, and perhaps even more so, that the veritable virtue of these studies is to instill confidence in their legitimacy. Such practitioners are masters in their domain; they have the right to speak, and the others have only to listen. They are not paralyzed by the idea of a level of competence that is officially greater than their own.

8
Pausanias Entrapped

But does Pausanias actually believe in the cultural myths that he reports on every page? Toward the end of his work, it will be recalled, he reveals that until that time he had considered the many legends that the Greeks had told him about the gods as so many examples of naïveté. However, he repeated them—sometimes, as we know, with criticism, or sometimes without, and this second case was by far the more frequent one. Did he accept everything he did not criticize, and was he a believing soul, or was he a Voltairean spirit who demolished some myths in order to undermine the foundations of all? We are going to return to the ''Pausanias question,'' for it has the merit of being complicated, and at the same time it shows the narrowness of the program within which the most sincere minds were struggling. For in the last part of his work, Pausanias is struggling.

For clarity's sake, it is better for us to begin with a summary of our conclusions. Pausanias exhibits a certain rationalism, but one that is not our own. In another connection, he is sometimes a historian, talking about what really was, and sometimes a philologist, whose task it is to tell what is said. Far from being Voltairean, his criticism of myth is proof that he had an elevated idea of the gods. Therefore, piety led him personally to condemn the majority of the legends that he related. Only, working more as a philologist than a historian, he often narrates these tales without judging them. Or else he is drawn into the game and speaks from the mythographic perspective, in the manner of our historians of philosophy who see and judge everything from the point of view of the thinker they are studying, including the more or less coherent details of the thinker's own doctrine. As for legendary history and genealogies, Pausanias reports them faithfully but accepts only the major points. What remains in his sieve is entirely comparable to what Thucydides retained in his Archeology.

Genealogical and etiological inventions that fool only those who wish to be charmed shock him less than absurdities concerning the gods. Such is his attitude up until the end of book 7. It continues to exist in the final three books, after he found his road to Damascus in Arcadia, but henceforth he wonders if there is not sometimes an allegorical or even a literal truth in the legends that once scandalized him. Nothing in all this will surprise our readers; but since Pausanias is a reticent author with a light touch, the case is not always easy to unravel. Pausanias has personality (much more than a Strabo, for example).

Two or three times, he lets the pen fall. "I omit the miraclous," he writes, and, refusing to tell the fable of Medusa, he gives two rational versions and cannot choose between them: Medusa was a queen killed in a war; Medusa was a monstrous beast such as still can be seen in the Sahara, according to the testimony of a Carthaginian historian.[175] Political or physical rationalization of myth. Three or four other times he enjoys himself; in Mantinea you can see a deer, now very old, wearing a collar that says, "I was a fawn when captured, at the time when /Agapenor went to Troy."[176] This proves that deer live even longer than elephants. His humor conceals his exasperation at seeing the Hellenes as naïve as the barbarians.[177] He ends up admitting[178] that fables seem to him to emerge from pure and simple naïveté, and sometimes he refuses to accept his responsibility: "I repeat the current Greek legend," he writes.[179]

But in the great majority of cases he suspends judgment. Indeed, he confines himself to reporting what the Greeks say, and for a long time this furnished a specific program of truth in which he could take shelter, no matter what his personal feelings were. We guess what this program was when we read what Dionysius of Halicarnassus writes in his *Judgment on Thucydides* about the historians of the fifth century:

> They have only one aim, which never varies: to bring to the knowledge of all men everything they could collect in the manner of memories belonging to different cities and that the local people had kept or to which temple monuments had been dedicated. They do not add or take away anything. Among these memories were myths that had been believed throughout the centuries, as well as fanciful adventures that seem very childish in our day.

These old historians did not, as our folklorists do, collect local traditions they did not believe, nor did they refrain from condemning them out of respect for foreign beliefs: they considered them to be truths, but truths that belonged to them no more than to anyone else. They belonged to the people of the country, for the natives are the best placed to know the truth about themselves; this truth about their city above all belongs to them by the same right as the city to which it pertains. This is a kind of principle of noninterference in the public truths of another.

Six centuries later, Pausanias still could imitate their neutrality because myths still maintained and always will maintain a lofty cultural dignity. Fable was not folklore, any more than the athletic contests at Olympia or elsewhere were spectacles to please the crowd;[180] they were national customs. There are many possibile definitions of folklore, and one of them evaluates it not on the basis of internal criteria but on the fact that it is rejected from the circle of a culture that considers itself the good and true one. Pausanias does not reject the national traditions embodied in myths. He also respects his own work, for his vocation is to gather the curiosities of each city, its legends and monuments. And to be ironic about what one studies shows little grace and bad conscience. Thus he dips his pen into his authors' inkwells and enters into their spirit. He often happens to declare that a particular version of a legend is more probable than another. Let us beware of always believing that he is speaking for himself in such cases.[181] He is speaking as a philologist who puts himself in his author's position and applies his auctorial criteria to him.

The rationalist criticism of myth, then, is followed by criticism based on internal unity. The inhabitants of Pheneüs say that Odysseus, who had lost his horses, found them while passing through the region and that he raised a bronze statue to Poseidon. It is plausible to believe in the legend but not in the statue, for, in the time of Odysseus, people still did not know how to cast bronze.[182] Sometimes the two criticisms are juxtaposed. The legend of Narcissus, who died because he loved his own image and was transformed into the flower that bears his name, is the result "of a total naïveté," because it is not natural for an already grown boy to be unable to distinguish reality from its image and because the narcissus existed well before that time. Everyone knows that Kore was playing with just such a flower in the field where Hades overtook her and carried her off to the Underworld.[183] When Pausanias thus applies to a myth the need for the internal consistency that reality obeys, one cannot conclude that he believes in its historicity. How many philologists, who do not believe in the historicity of Trimalchio or that of Lady Macbeth, confuse fiction and reality no less and force Petronius and Shakespeare to compete with real life?[184] They wish to determine the exact season of Trimalchio's banquet and resolve textual contradictions in which fruits from different seasons are placed together; they wish to establish the exact number of Lady Macbeth's children. Nonetheless, Pausanias does not believe in the reality of Hades and the historicity of the rape of Kore. We have already seen that, according to him, "It is not easy to believe that the gods possess any underground dwelling. . . ."

As a philologist, Pausanias tacitly accepts all the legends he does not criticize, but as a man he challenges them. Callisto, Zeus's beloved, was not transformed into a constellation, since the Arcadians point out her tomb. This is an example of the requirement for internal consistency, and it is the philologist who speaks. "I repeat here what the Greeks say," he had stipulated at first. Here is the man peering out from behind the role and keeping his distance from a ridiculous and impious legend. One thus concludes that all Zeus did was give the name of Callisto to the constellation. Here we see the rationalist historian acting on the philologist's orders and offering a believable interpretation of a myth in whose historicity the man does not believe.[185] Pausanias has a clear mind and a subtle style.

It is piety that keeps Pausanias from believing most of the legends he faithfully assembles. We have to dissociate demythologization from irreligion. At this time, disbelief was recognized not in criticism of myths but in criticism of oracles. Cicero, Oenomaus, and Diogenianus are certainly not pious souls.[186] By heaping ridicule on oracles, they did not for an instant claim to exonerate the gods. Pausanias himself does believe in the gods and even in their miracles: for him the "epiphany" of the divinity at Delphi at the time of the Galatian invasion is an indubitable fact.[187]

The minor revolution affecting Pausanias on the occasion of his research on Arcadian antiquities consisted in his realizing that some legends, far from slandering the gods, could have an elevated meaning.[188] He had already become a partisan of the "physical" (as it was called) interpretation of the gods. While visiting the temple of Aegium, he met a Phoenician who had told him that Asclepius was the air and Apollo the sun, because air and sun procure health, and he had agreed.[189] But while he is in the process of studying Arcadia, he furthermore imagines the possibility of an allegorical exegesis, since the sages of yore "had the habit of speaking in riddles." The amazing story told by the Arcadians of Rhea giving Cronos a foal to deceive him and thereby saving Poseidon from this ogre of a father must not be foolishness; it has some deep meaning, physical or perhaps theological.[190] Such was the first step: to cease taking the myths literally.[191]

The second step was more remarkable: to abandon the principle of current things and admit that in mythical times conditions could have been different from our own. An Arcadian legend said in fact that Lycaon was changed into a wolf for having sacrificed an infant to Zeus. "I for my part believe this story," writes Pausanias. "It has been a legend among the Arcadians from of old, and it has the additional merit of probability. For the men of those days, because of their righteousness and piety, were guests of the gods, eating at the same board. The good were openly honored by the gods, and sinners were openly visited by their wrath."[192] And so in these far-off days it was possible to see men raised to the stature of gods. Why not? Epicurus, a man of few superstitions and convinced that the world was very young and still in the process of attaining its full form (it is only in this sense that he believed in "progress"), concluded from this that over a few centuries the world had undergone considerable transformations.[193] He admitted that men of olden times, more vigorous than those of today, had eyes good enough to see the gods in broad daylight, while now we can manage to capture only the emissions of their atoms through the channel of dreams.

Pausanias himself, we see, deliberately relates his evolution to what he learned in Arcadia and believes the legend of Lycaon because the tradition for it is extremely ancient.[194] It is not one of those imaginings that later come to cover up the original truth. First, it must be recalled that Pausanias is without superstition but not at all without religion. Moreover, skipping over three or four centuries of mythology that had become the province of the learned, he reestablished contact, bookish but not banal, with the local life of unknown legends. He scours the libraries, and the old books make him think. Arcadia, too. This rough, poor country, so unidyllic, with its archaic character, had already led Callimachus to dream. It had the reputation for not changing any of its original customs and beliefs. Pausanias is very sensitive to archaism, which leads to the truth. We have a strange proof of it. From the time of his youthful work on Athens, Pausanias had held in high regard the hymns of a certain Pamphos, whom the moderns place in the Hellenistic period and whom Pausanias believed to be more ancient than Homer himself.[195] Now we see him thinking that Pamphos was educated among the Arcadians. In short, overcome by the foolishness of so many myths, but, good Greek that he was and unable to imagine that it would be possible to lie about everything to everyone, Pausanias finally admitted that myths sometimes told the truth by allegory and riddle and that sometimes they told the truth literally, for they were so old that one could not suspect them of being distorted by lies. Is this a mental revolution? I do not know. As an evolution it is perfectly logical.

It is an evolution remaining within the lines of Greek thought as it had existed since the time of Thucydides and Plato. In his piety as well as his uneasiness, Pausanias remains classical, and nothing in him leads us to foretell the future birth of Neoplatonism and religiosity. Nevertheless Pausanias is not an easy author, and I must admit my own uncertainties to the reader. If it is possible to untangle the threads of the complicated woof woven by our author, it still remains difficult to decide in matters of detail whether he is speaking on his own account or only as a philologist. Here the Arcadians—yes, the Arcadians—tell him that the battle of the gods and the Giants took place in their country on the banks of the Alpheus. Is he going to begin believing in these tales of the Giants, of which Xenophanes had already heard enough? He refers to arguments taken from natural history; he discusses the matter at some length.[196] Is he playing the game, or does he really believe? I give up on deciding the case. Another time, in Chaeronea, someone shows him Agamemnon's scepter, which had been forged by Hephaestus in person, as is told in the *Iliad*.[197] He discusses this relic for some time, and, eliminating other works claimed to be by Hephaestus by dating them according to stylistic criteria, he concludes: "So probably the scepter is the only work of Hephaestus." If this passage were not in book 9, one would see in it the attitude of a philologist who pretends to believe everything, but with a dash of wit. Except that, since Pausanias told us in book 8 that, in these ancient centuries, the gods mixed in the affairs of men, I no longer know what to think. Nor am I any more certain regarding a third case, the genealogy of the kings of Arcadia; for when he speaks of history, Pausanias displays the same sincerity and craftiness as when he speaks of religious legends.[198] Let us make a leap and admit that he does it deliberately. This Greek, who has been taken for a compiler, a kind of Baedeker, takes pleasure in plunging us into doubt, as Valéry or the late Jean Paulhan would. Let us say, rather, as Callimachus would; for the humor of the Alexandrians was just that.

Pausanias the historian: his method is the same as it is for religious myths, and our doubts are sometimes the same (the genealogy of the kings of Arcadia . . .). Does he take responsibility for another outlandish tale, that of the kings of Achaea? In religion he believes in the divinities but not in mythology, and in history he believes in the global authenticity of heroic times. Only his notion of the global is not our own. It is that of Thucydides when the latter writes that Hellen gave his name to the Hellenes and that Atreus, who was the uncle of Eurystheus, flattered the people and became king. What is authentic are the principal characters and the political facts. And the proper names.

There is indeed a passage where at last it seems possible to discern what Pausanias thinks, and we give it here for clarity:

> The Boeotians as a race got their name from Boeotus, who, *legend says,* was the son of Itonus and the nymph Melanippe, and grandson of Amphictyon. The cities are called in some cases after men, but in most after women. The Plataeans were originally, *in my opinion,* sprung from the soil; their name comes from Plataea, whom *they consider* to be a daughter of the river Asopus. *It is clear* that the Plataeans too were of old ruled by kings; for everywhere in Greece, in ancient times, kingship and not democracy was the established form of government. But the Plataeans *know* of no king except Asopus and Cithaeron before him, *holding* that the latter gave his name to the mountain, the former to the river. *I think* that Plataea also, after whom the city is named, was a daughter of King Asopus, and not of the river.[199]

If one wishes to know the past of a city, one asks the natives in hopes that they will have a detailed memory of it, and there is no reason to question these memories, except for the puerilities—nymphs and river-fathers—which can easily be corrected. Livy did not question the authenticity of the list of the kings of Rome (he questioned only the biased fables before Romulus). Why would Pausanias question the royal lists of Arcadia or Achaea?

9
Forger's Truth, Philologist's Truth

No, he did not question these imaginary lists, which had duped so many people, beginning with their own creators. This historiography of sincere forgers is so strange that it is worth considering for a moment. We will see that if we pursue this problem of the forger, it becomes impossible to distinguish between the imaginary and the real.

Of all the peculiar notions that we have examined since the beginning of this book and that constitute what is commonly known as Greek Reason, this is without doubt the strangest: in it fiction acquires brute materiality. How does one decide that a king was called Ampyx? Why this name instead of a million others? A program of truth existed in which it was accepted that someone, Hesiod or someone else, told the truth when he reeled off the names that passed through his mind or spouted the most unbridled Swedenborgian fantasies. For such people psychological imagination is a source of veracity.

This attitude, normal in the founder of a religion, is not incomprehensible in a historian, either. Historians are merely prophets in reverse, and they flesh out and animate their *post eventum* predictions with imaginative flourishes. This is called "historical retrodiction" or "synthesis," and this imaginative faculty furnishes three-fourths of any page of history, with documents providing the rest. There is more. History is also a novel containing deeds and proper names, and we have seen that, while reading, we believe that what we read is true. Only afterward do we call it fiction, and even then we must belong to a society in which the idea of fiction obtains.

Why shouldn't a historian invent the names of his heroes? A novelist does. Neither one invents in the strict sense of the word. They discover in their imagination a name they had not thought of before. The mythographer who made up the list of the kings of Arcadia thereby discovered in himself a foreign reality that he had not deliberately put there and that had not been there beforehand. He was in the state of mind in which a novelist finds himself when his characters "get away from him." He was able to let himself follow this reality, since in those days people did not have the habit of asking historians, "What are your sources?"

As for the reader . . . One can expect pleasure or information from a narrative; the account itself can pass for true or fictional. In the first case, one can believe it or deem it the lie of a forger. The *Iliad* passed largely for history, but, since readers expected entertainment, the poet could add his own inventions without disturbing them. On the other hand, readers of Castor, the inventive historian of the long line of legendary kings of Argos, consulted him for information, and instead of floating in pleasure—which is neither true nor false—they believed it all. But that is precisely the issue. The very boundary between information and entertainment is dictated by convention, and societies other than ours have practiced agreeable sciences. For the ancients, one of these sciences was mythology, which was viewed as part of "grammar" or erudition. There one savored the heady pleasures of learning, the delights of dilettantism. When the parent of a student, clever and well read, asked his son's grammarian sticky questions concerning "the name of Anchises' nurse or Anchemolus' stepmother," as Juvenal puts it, he cares little about the historicity of the two. Even we moderns may take pleasure in history as a detective story, and underneath its academic presentation the strange work of Carcopino, beginning with his big book on Virgil and Ostia, is largely born out of fiction-history.

As a matter of fact, the problem is to distinguish fiction-history from history that is meant to be serious. Are these works to be judged on the basis of their truth? The most serious of scholars can make a mistake, and, above all, fiction is not error. According to rigor? The rigor is just as great in the work of a forger, whose imagination unwittingly follows the dictates of a program of truth just as predetermined as that blindly followed by the "serious" historian; furthermore, it is sometimes the very same program. On the basis of the psychic processes they engage? They are the same ones: scientific invention is not a faculty pertaining only to the soul; it is the same thing as invention pure and simple. On the criteria of the society to which the historian belongs? Here is where the shoe pinches the tightest, for what conforms to the program of truth in one society will be perceived as imposture or elucubration in another. A forger is a man working in the wrong century.

The day that Jacques de Voragine, known above all as the author of *The Golden Legend,* discovered the Trojan origins of the town of Genoa in his imagination, or the day that one of Frédégaire's predecessors found in his mind those of the Frankish monarchy, they were only doing the reasonable thing: they were forming synthetic judgments based on the *a priori* of a program of their time. We have seen that a whole empire was founded by the descendants of Aeneas (Francion, in this case) and that every land (Francia, in this case) took its name from a man. It still needed to be explained what this son of Aeneas could have been doing on the Frisian coast, the original land of the Franks. Frédégaire's answer is no more hypothetical and no less based on serious indicators than our own hypotheses concerning the origin of the Etruscans or the obscure days of Rome.

For everything there is a season, however. The ancient genealogists could invent the names of gods or ancient kings. Everyone understood that heretofore unobtainable myths had come down to them. But in 1743 one of Vasari's Neapolitan emulators concocted all of a piece the existence, names, and dates of the artists of southern Italy; he was taken for a mythomaniac when the falsification was exposed one hundred and fifty years later. For, by 1890, art history had other programs—which are academic and outmoded today.

Let us make a distinction, then, between the alleged forgers, who are only doing what their contemporaries find normal but who amuse posterity, and forgers who are regarded as such in the eyes of their contemporaries. To take our examples from the small fry, let us say that the second case is that of a character at whom it is better to laugh than cry, particularly since he never existed, all proofs of his reality being questionable. An impostor took his place before the tribunals; his books were written by others, and the supposed eyewitnesses to his existence were either prejudiced or the victims of a collective hallucination. Once we know that he did not exist, the scales fall from our eyes, and we then see that the supposed proofs of his reality are false. It was enough not to have any preconceived ideas. This mythical creature was called Faurisson. If his legend is to be believed, after penning obscure lucubrations on the subject of Rimbaud and Lautréamont, he achieved some notoriety in 1980 by maintaining that

Auschwitz never existed. He was roundly castigated. I protest that the poor man was close to his truth. He was close, as a matter of fact, to a type of crank that historians who study the past two centuries sometimes encounter: anticlericals who deny the historicity of Christ (which irritates me, atheist that I am) and addled brains who deny the existence of Socrates, Joan of Arc, Shakespeare, or Molière, get excited about Atlantis, or discover monuments erected by extraterrestrials on Easter Island. In another millennium, Faurisson could have had a fine career as a mythologist or, even three centuries ago, as an astrologer. Some lack in his personality or inventiveness kept him from being a psychoanalyst. He had a taste for glory nonetheless, like the author of these lines or any other well-born soul. Unfortunately, there was a misunderstanding between him and his admirers. The latter failed to recognize that, since truth is plural (as we like to think we have established), Faurisson was speaking from the perspective of a mythical rather than historical truth. Since truth is also analogical, these readers believed that they and Faurisson were operating according to the same program that produced other books relating to Auschwitz; they naïvely compared his book to these others. Faurisson made their confusion easier by imitating the method of these books, possibly by means of operations which, in the jargon of the historians whose methods had their roots in legal controversy, were called falsifications of historical truth.

The only mistake Faurisson made was to place himself on his adversaries' ground. Instead of asserting everything from scratch, as the historian Castor did, he claimed to take part in a debate. With his systematized mania for interpretation, he questioned everything, but unilaterally; he gave them the rope with which to hang him. Either he had to believe in the gas chambers or doubt everything, like the Taoists who wondered if they were not butterflies dreaming that they were humans and that there were gas chambers . . . But like his opponents, Faurisson wanted to be right; hyperbolic doubt concerning the entire universe was not his purpose.

Let us leave this little man to his little obsessions. The paradox of the forger (one is always the forger of another program) is completely over his head. This paradox requires distinguishing between error—what the seventeenth century attributed to psychological imagination—and the historical vagaries of truth, or what the constitutive imagination posits as truth. It requires one to make a distinction between the forger who takes advantage of his program and the outsider who is using another one. Hesiod was not a forger when he found all the names of the daughters of the sea in his head. Does a kernel of acquired facts, which could be the object of a cumulative progress, persist across successive programs?

The discussion of facts always takes place within a program. Naturally, anything can happen, and perhaps we will one day discover that the Greek texts are a fully fashioned forgery perpetrated by the scholars of the sixteenth century. But this excessive doubt, one-way in Faurisson's case, and this ever-present potential for error are one thing. Empty skepticism is not to be confused with the avowal that no program predominates. A century and a half ago people still believed in the Flood; fifteen centuries ago, they believed in myths.

It is clear that the existence or the nonexistence of Theseus and gas chambers in one point in space and time has a material reality that owes nothing to our imagination. But this reality or irreality is perceived, misunderstood, or interpreted in one way or another according to the program in force. It, by itself, does not claim our attention; things are not perfectly clear. The same is true of the programs themselves. A good program does not naturally come into view. There is no truth of things, nor is it immanent.

In order to reject myth or the Flood, it is not enough to study more attentively or develop a better method. It is necessary to change programs. What was built awry cannot be rebuilt. One finds another house. For matters of *facts* are recognizable only in the form of an interpretation. I do not mean that facts do not exist. Materiality certainly exists; it is in the act. However, as old Duns Scotus says, it is not the act of nothing. The materiality of the gas chambers does not automatically lead to the knowledge one can have about them. Each is distinct; yet, for us, matters of *facts* and interpretation are always tied together, like those referendums in which de Gaulle asked the voters for one answer to two different questions.

In other words, the errors of a certain program—that of a Faurisson or a Carcopino, for example—are added to the vagaries of all programs. We cannot separate imaginations from Imagination. In the words of Heidegger in the *Holzwege,* ''The reserve of a being can be refusal or be nothing but dissimulation.'' Vagaries or error: ''We never have the direct certainty of knowing whether it is one or the other.'' We know how Heidegger has imposed the idea on our time that beings remain in a reserve. They appear only in a flash, a clearing, and each time we believe that this clearing is limitless. Beings exist for us in a self-evident modality. In this clearing one could see a plain and say that there is no forest all around it, that nothing exists outside of what our imagination constitutes, that our programs, far from being limited, are supplements that we add to being. But Heidegger, on the contrary, thinks that the clearing is not everything, and this leads him finally to discover a background of truth, even a truth that is occasionally badly frayed, which leaves historians, and not only them, speculating. (''One way in which truth unfolds its presence is in the installation of a State.'') We suspect that a little historical and sociological criticism is worth more than a lot of ontology.

A forger is a fish who, for reasons of temperament, has ended up in the wrong bowl. His scientific imagination follows myths no longer found on the program. That this program is often, indeed always, as imaginary as the one followed by the forger, I willingly believe. But there are two types of imagination, one of which decrees the programs, while the other serves to execute them. The latter, the well-known faculty discussed by psychologists, is intrahistorical. The first, or constitutive imagination, is not an individual creative gift; it is a kind of objective spirit in which individuals are socialized. It forms the sides of each bowl, which are imaginary or arbitrary, for a thousand different boundaries have been and will continue to be created through the ages. It is not transhistorical but interhistorical. All this eliminates any way of making a profound distinction between cultural works that are intended to be true and the pure products of the imagination. We will return to this point, but first let us give the brief epilogue of our plot.

The birth of historical science as the moderns have imagined it was not made possible by the distinction between primary and secondary sources (which was noted very early on and is no panacea); it was made possible by the distinction between sources and reality, between historians and historical facts. After the time of Pausanias there is more and more confusion between the two, and it will continue for a long time, as far as Bossuet, who could still establish a synchronicity between Abimelech and Hercules because he was repeating what he found in Eusebius' *Chronicle*. It is with this new way of believing in myths that we will end.

The relations between the historical genre and what for a long time was called grammar or philology are not simple. History wishes to know "what truly took place," *was eigentlich geschehen ist* (said Ranke),[200] while philology is thought about thought, knowledge of what is known, *Erkenntnis des Erkannten* (said Boeckh).[201]

Often, knowledge of what happened is only a means of explaining a classical text, a noble object of which history is only the referent. This is the case when the history of the Roman Republic serves only to provide a better understanding of Cicero. More often, the two objects are confused. What used to be called "literary history" (i.e., history known through literature) and today is called humanism views Cicero through the events of the final century of the Republic and regards the history of the century in light of the innumerable details contained in Cicero's work.[202] The reverse of this attitude is more rare, but it also exists. It consists in using a text to illustrate the reality to which it refers—a reality which, for the historian-philologist, remains the principal objective. This is the attitude of a Strabo. We know of Strabo's blind love for Homer, which was founded on the example of his master, Chrysippus. This love is present to such a degree that book 8 of his *Geography,* which contains the description of Greece, is principally concerned with identifying the place names found in Homer. Was Strabo aiming for a better understanding of Homer's text or, on the contrary, was he trying to exalt the various cities by giving them a Homeric reference? The second interpretation is the only valid one; otherwise, the following sentence would be incomprehensible: "But three of the cities mentioned by the poet, 'Rhipē and Stratiē, and windy Enispē,' are not only hard to find, but are of no use to any who find them, because they are deserted."[203]

But a third attitude, extremely widespread, also exists, one in which no attempt is made to distinguish between reality and the text that speaks of it. This is already the attitude of this Eusebius through whose offices mythical history, such as we find it in a Pausanias, has been passed on to Bossuet. Not that Eusebius was incapable of distinguishing an event from a text! However, for him, sources themselves are part of history; to be a historian is to narrate history, and it is also to give an account of historians. Don't the majority of our philosophers and our psychoanalysts do the same thing in their respective domains? Most often to be a philosopher is to be a historian of philosophy. To know philosophy is to know what the different philosophers thought they knew. To know what the Oedipus complex is consists first of all in knowing or commenting on what Freud said about it.

To be more exact, in this blurring between the book and the things the book is about, the emphasis is sometimes on the things, at others it is on the book itself. The first case is that of any text regarded as revelation or revelatory. To comment on Aristotle, Marx, or the *Digest,* to study a text thoroughly, to assume that it has unity or to credit it beforehand with the most intelligent or up-to-date interpretation, means assuming that the text has the depth and consistency of reality itself. Henceforth, deepening one's understanding of the text will be the same as deepening one's understanding of reality.[204] The text will be said to be profound because it will be impossible to mine it beyond what the author has written. What is unearthed in this fashion is confused with the things themselves.

But the emphasis can also be on the book seen as an object of corporate superstition. This is the attitude that in Antiquity was ascribed to philologists, who were called grammarians. This view was not limited to considering as classic those texts whose assertions, whether true or false, were in any case important to know. What the book said was deemed authentic. As a result, a grammarian might happen to present, as true, legends that he did not personally believe in. There is a story that the greatest scholar of Antiquity, Didymus, who had written more books than he could remember, became angry one day when someone told him a historical anecdote that in Didymus' opinion had no foundation.[205] He relented when he was shown one of his own works in which the tale was said to be true.

This outlook differs from the attitude of myth, in which the word speaks as if vested with its own authority. It also differs from the perspective of a Thucydides, a Polybius, or a Pausanias. Like our modern reporters, they do not cite their sources and seem to want to be taken at their word, for they write for the public rather than for their colleagues. Nor does Eusebius cite his sources; he transcribes them. This is not because he takes them at face value or even less because he is the first to embody "truly scientific" history. What is written forms a part of what is to be known. Eusebius does not make a distinction between knowing things and knowing what is in books. He confuses history and grammar, and, if one believes in progress, one would have to say that his method is a step backward.[206]

A similar attitude, governed by a need to know what is known, was

well suited to the conservation of myths. A fine example is Pliny's
Natural History. Here is a list of great inventions: the theory of the
winds we owe to Aeolus; the invention of towers, "to the Cyclopes,
according to Aristotle"; botany, to Chiron, son of Saturn; astronomy,
to Atlas; and wheat, to Ceres, "who, for that, was deemed a
goddess."[207] As often happens, the method, in this case the
questionnaire, generated the results. Pliny succumbed to the law of the
genre. Instead of thinking about the things themselves, this
indefatiguable reader rose to the challenge of answering the question,
"Do we know who invented what?" And he answered, "Aeolus,
Atlas," for he knew everything found in all the books.

Eusebius does the same thing. His *Chronological Tables or
Summary of All Histories* sums up nine centuries of thought
concerning myth and will serve as the basis for historical knowledge
up to and including the work of Dom Calmet.[208] Here we find
genealogies: of the kings of Sicyon and Argos, of whom the first was
Inachus, the source being Castor the historian; that of Mycenae, with
Atreus, Thyestes, and Orestes; and that of Athens, with Cecrops and
Pandion. We see every possible synchronism: during Abimelech's
reign over the Hebrews the battle took place between the Lapiths and
the Centaurs—the latter of whom "Palaephatus, in his *Things Not To
Be Believed,* said had been famous Thessalonian knights." We have
the dates: Medea followed Jason and left her father Aeëtes 780 years
after Abraham and, consequently, 1,235 years before the birth of
Christ. Eusebius is a rationalist. In the year 650 of Abraham,
Ganymede was carried off by a prince of the region: thus, this Zeus
with his bird of prey was a "mere fable." The Gorgon, whose head
Perseus cut off in the year 670 of Abraham, was purely and simply a
courtesan of fascinating beauty. Let us end by once again quoting the
Discours sur l'histoire universelle by the Bishop of Meaux: the Trojan
War, "The fifth age of the world," is a "time suited for bringing
together what the fabled times," where truth is "clothed" in
falsehoods, "have of the most certain and most beautiful." As a
matter of fact, "there one sees the Achilles, the Agamemnons, the
Menelaus, the Ulysses, Sarpedon, the son of Jupiter, Aeneas, the son
of Venus."

From Herodotus to Pausanias and Eusebius—I was going to say, to
Bossuet—the Greeks continued to believe in and grapple with myth,
and their ideas about the fundamental nature of the problem and even

possible solutions developed very little. During half a millennium there were many, such as Carneades, Cicero, and Ovid, who did not believe in the gods, but no one questioned Heracles and Aeolus, even at the cost of rationalization. The Christians expelled the gods, in whom no one believed, from mythology, but they said nothing of the mythological heroes, for they believed in them as much as everyone else did, including Aristotle, Polybius, and Lucretius.[209]

How did it come about that people finally ceased believing in the historicity of Aeolus, Heracles, and Perseus? Neither sound scientific method nor dialectic, materialist or not, had any part in it. It is rare for great political or intellectual problems to lead to a solution and be resolved, ordered, and surpassed. More often they are lost in the shifting sands, where they are forgotten or erased. Christianization eliminated a problem for which the Greeks had not found the solution and which they were unable to abandon. It is permitted to imagine that they were enthralled with it for reasons that were no less accidental.

Thus, though centuries had passed since nursemaids had spoken to children about heroes and gods, the learned still believed in them in their way. They ceased believing for two reasons. History, born of inquiry and reportage, had, with Eusebius, come to be confused with philology. A very different thing, which also bears the name history, arises with the moderns. It is the product of controversy and a divorce from philology. Respect no longer led to confusing historical reality with the texts that narrate it at the same time that the Quarrel of the Ancients and the Moderns deprived these texts of their aura. Then along came Fontenelle, who thought that myth could not contain one word of truth. Such changes did not do away with the problem of myth, which instead became more serious.[210] People no longer asked, "What truth does myth have? For it contains some truth, since nothing cannot speak of nothing." Now they asked, "What meaning or function does myth have? For one cannot speak or imagine for nothing." In truth.

This need to find a justification for mythmaking betrays our own uneasiness about error and is the obverse of our own mythology of truth and knowledge. How can humanity, we think, have been so hugely mistaken for so long? Myth versus reason, error versus truth: the odds should be one out of two. Since truth remains unique and above suspicion, the fault must lie with modalities of belief of unequal value and intensity. Perhaps humanity was wrong to be swayed for so long by the argument of authority or by collective representations. But did it truly believe in them? Voltairean minds are secretly inclined to doubt that their neighbor truly believes in all this nonsense. They sense hypocrisy in every belief. They are not completely wrong. People do not believe in neutrons, myths, or anti-Semitism in the same way they believe in the evidence of the senses and the morality of the tribe, for truth is not single. But these truths are nonetheless analogical (they seem to be the same), and they are equally genuine, since they make their proponents act equally strongly. The plurality of modalities of belief is in reality the plurality of the criteria for truth.

This truth is the child of the imagination. The authenticity of our beliefs is not measured according to the truth of their object. Again we must understand the reason, which is a simple one: it is we who fabricate our truths, and it is not "reality" that makes us believe. For "reality" is the child of the constitutive imagination of our tribe. If it were otherwise, the quasi-totality of universal culture would be inexplicable—mythologies, doctrines, pharmacopoeias, false and spurious sciences. As long as we speak of the truth, we will understand nothing of culture and will never manage to attain the same perspective on our culture as we have on past centuries, when people spoke of gods and myths.

The Greeks offer the example of a millennial failure to tear themselves away from a lie. They were never able to say, "Myth is completely false, since it rests on nothing." Bossuet will not say it, either. The imaginary itself is never challenged, as if some secret sense of foreboding warned that, if it were, no more truths would remain. Either people forget the myths of olden times in order to speak of other things and enter a different imaginative domain, or else they absolutely want to find the kernel of truth that lies hidden in myth or makes it speak.

We will observe the same thing if we move from the heroic myths, which are the only ones we have examined, to belief in gods in the strict sense of the term. In *Atheism in Pagan Antiquity,* A. B. Drachmann has shown that ancient atheism did not so much deny the existence of the gods as it criticized the popular idea of the deities. It did not exclude a more philosophical conception of divinity. In their own way, the Christians went no further in their negation of the pagan gods. They did not call the myths "vain fables" so much as term them "unworthy conceptions." Since they wished to put their god in place of the pagan gods, it is possible to think that the whole project would first entail showing that Zeus did not exist and then setting forth proofs for the existence of God. This was not their program. They seem less to censure the pagan gods for not existing than to reproach them for not being good ones. They seem less hasty to deny Zeus than to replace him with a king more worthy of occupying the divine throne. This is why the apologetics of ancient Christianity leave such a strange impression. It seems that, to establish God, it was enough to banish the other gods. The desire was not so much to destroy false ideas as to supplant them. Even where the Christians seem to attack paganism on the subject of its veracity, they do nothing of the sort. As we saw earlier, they uselessly criticized the puerility and immorality of mythological accounts in which the pagans had never believed and that had nothing in common with the elevated or sophisticated conception that later paganism had of the divinity. The goal of this polemic was not to persuade an adversary but to banish all rivals and make it felt that the jealous God would tolerate no competition, unlike the pagan gods, who all tolerated one another (for all were true, and no one excluded the others). It mattered little that the attacks against the gods of fable were irrelevant; what was important was to make it understood that no logic of appeasement would be tolerated. The pagan gods were unworthy, and that was that. Their unworthiness undoubtedly implied their falseness, but the implication that carried more weight than this intellectual viewpoint was, above all, that people no longer wished to hear about them. They did not deserve to exist. If some thinking person's scruple makes it necessary to translate this unworthiness into doctrine, one will say with Eusebius that the pagan gods are not untrue gods but falsified gods: they are demons that have passed themselves off as gods in order to mislead men, particularly by their knowledge of the future. They have impressed men with veracious oracles.

It is less difficult to eliminate a product of the imagination than to deny it. It is very difficult to deny a god, even if it is the god of others. Even ancient Judaism managed it with difficulty; it asserted that foreign gods were not as strong as the national god or else that they were not interesting: disdain or horror, not negation. But to a patriot they amount to the same thing. Do the gods of others exist? Their existence is of little importance. What matters is that the gods of others are worthless; they are wooden or stone idols who have ears so they cannot hear. These are the gods that people "have not known"; they are the gods "whom he had not given unto them," repeats Deuteronomy, and the most ancient books are more openly explicit. When the Ark was placed in the temple of Dagon, the following morning the idol of this Dagon, god of the Philistines, was found face down, prostrate before the god of Israel. The Book of Samuel tells the story, and Psalm 96 will say, "All gods bow down before Yaweh." One desires to know the gods of other nations only through international dealings. When it is said to the Amorrhean, "Why would you not possess what Camos, your god, gives you to possess?" it is a way of promising to respect his territory. Nations easily dispense with the notion of true and false, which is practiced or thought to be practiced only by certain intellectuals at certain periods of history.

If we think about it for a moment, the idea that truth does not exist is no more paradoxical or paralyzing than the idea of a perpetually provisional scientific truth that will be proved false tomorrow. The myth of science impresses us. But do not confuse science with its scholasticism. Science finds no truths, either mathematized or formalized; it discovers unknown facts that can be interpreted in a thousand ways. The discovery of a subatomic particle, a successful technical recipe, or the DNA molecule is no more sublime than the discovery of infusoria, the Cape of Good Hope, the New World, or the anatomy of an organ . . . or Sumerian civilization. Sciences are no more serious than the humanities, and since, in history, facts are not separable from interpretation and one can imagine all the interpretations one wishes, the same must be true in the exact sciences.

10
The Need to Choose between Culture and Belief in a Truth

Therefore, people believed in myths for a long time, according to programs that, to be sure, varied enormously from one era to another. It is normal for people to believe in the works of the imagination. People believe in religions, in *Madame Bovary* while they read, in Einstein, in Fustel de Coulanges, in the Trojan origins of the Franks. However, in certain societies some of these works are deemed fictions. The realm of the imaginary is not limited to these, however. Politics, in the sense of political practices and not simply so-called ideologies, have the arbitrary and crushing inertia of established programs. In its political aspect, the "hidden part of the iceberg" of the ancient city lasted for nearly as long as myth. Beneath the capacious pseudo-classical drapery that our banal political rationalism lays over it, strange contours that belong only to this hidden realm can be detected. Daily life itself, far from being rooted in immediacy, is the crossroads of the imagination, and there people actively believe in racism and fortune-tellers. Empiricism and experimentation are negligible quantities. We will give imagination its due if we reflect that Einstein, to take a legendary example, has nothing earthbound about him. He erected a theoretical skyscraper that has yet to be tested. When this finally happens, the theory still will not be verified; it will only not have been invalidated.

This is not the worst. These successive dream palaces, all of which have passed for the truth, have the most varied styles of truth. The imagination that constitutes these styles has no order to its ideas; it follows the accidents of historic causality. This imagination not only moves from one plane to another but changes its very criteria. Far from being an indication that speaks for itself, truth is the most variable of all measures. It is not a transhistorical invariant but a work of the constitutive imagination. Whether men on either side of the

Pyrenees or either side of 1789 have different ideas is not very important. What is much more serious is that not only the very aim of our divergent assertions but our criteria and means of obtaining true ideas—in short, our programs—vary without our realizing it.

As Guy Lardreau has recently written, "To say that the transcendental is historically constituted amounts to saying that universality cannot be assigned to it; it is necessary to think of a *particular transcendental*. But, after all, there is nothing more mysterious than what is collectively called a culture."[211] The program of historical truth that informs the present book does not consist in saying how reason progresses, how France was built, or how society lived or thought about its foundations; it consists in reflecting on the constitution of the truth over the centuries and in looking back to see the course of the road that has been traveled. It is a product of reflectivity. It does not follow that this program is truer than the others and, even less, that it has more reasons for dominating and enduring than the others. What does follow is that we can say the following words here without contradicting ourselves: "The truth is that truth varies." In this Nietzschean conception the history of discourses and practices plays the role of a transcendental criticism.[212]

Constitutive imagination? These words do not designate a faculty of individual psychology but refer to the fact that each epoch thinks and acts within arbitrary and inert frameworks (it goes without saying that in a given century the programs of one sector of activity can contradict those of another and that these contradictions will for the most part go unnoticed). Once one is in one of these fishbowls, it takes genius to get out of it and innovate. On the other hand, once the work of genius has changed the fishbowl, children, starting in the primary grades, can be socialized into the new program. They will be as satisfied with it as their ancestors had been with theirs, and they will scarcely see a way of getting out of it, since they see nothing beyond it.[213] When one does not see what one does not see, one does not even see that one is blind. There is all the more reason for people to fail to recognize the irregular shape of these limits: we believe we live within natural boundaries. Furthermore, since the false analogy of truth has operated throughout the ages, we believe that our ancestors had already occupied the same homeland as we, or at least that the achievement of national unity had been foreshadowed and that some progress would complete it. If anything deserves the name of ideology, it is indeed truth.

Must it be repeated? This transcendental is *the fact that* things happen this way; it is the description of how they happen. It is not an authority or infrastructure that *makes things* happen this way. What would such a word game mean? We cannot claim, then, that this is reducing history to a process that is as implacable as it is irresponsible. I admit that irresponsibility is indeed an ugly thing and that, since it is ugly, it is surely false (Diodorus will tell you that). But, thank heaven, this is not the issue. The words "dormitive virtue" describe the effects of opium, which are explained by chemical causes. Programs of truth have historical causes. Their inertia, the slow pace with which they follow one another, is itself empirical. It is the result of what we call socialization (Nietzsche said "training," and this is the least racist and biological idea there is). This slowness, alas, is not the slow "labor" leading to the birth of the negative, which is also called the return of the repressed. It is not the shock of reality or the progress of reason and other responsible ideals. The constitution and succession of programs are explained by the same causes that historians are accustomed to treating, at least when they are not making sacrifices to predetermined schemes. Programs are built like buildings, with rows of succeeding blocks, each episode explained by the details of preceding episodes (individual inventiveness and the chances for the success that "takes" or not are possibly part of this polygon of innumerable causes). As a matter of fact, the construction of this edifice is not centered on great reasons, such as human nature, social needs, the logic of things that are what they are, or the forces of production. But we must not minimize the debate: a Marxist thinker of as high a stature as Habermas is not going to encumber himself with dormitive hypostases, such as forces or relations of production. He banishes them a word. But it is more difficult to banish reason. Habermas summarizes his philosophy somewhere with these words: "Man cannot fail to learn." That is the whole question, it seems to me. The opposition between Habermas and Foucault, i.e., Marx and Nietzsche, revives, in the age of the incoherent modern trinity of Marx-Freud-Nietzsche, the conflict between rationalism and irrationalism.[214]

Now all this is not without consequences for the current status of historical research. For forty or eighty years, the leading historiography has been based on an implicit program according to which the idea of writing history means writing the history of society. People hardly believe any more that there is such a thing as human nature, and they leave to political philosophers the idea that a truth of things exists. But they believe in society, and this enables them to account for the area between what is called economics and what can be put under the heading of ideology. But what, then, is to be done with all the rest? What is to be done with myth, with religions (when they have more than simply an ideological function), with all manner of far-fetched notions or, more simply, with art and science? It is quite simple. Either literary history, to return to this example, will be a part of social history, or, if it cannot or will not be a part of it, it is not history and its existence will be forgotten. It will be relegated to a specific category, that of historians of literature, who are historians in name only.

In this manner, the greater part of cultural and social life remains outside the field of historiography, even the historiography that is not concerned with events. Now, if one tries to account for this larger part in order one day to be able to open up the uninhabited regions that Lucien Febvre terms the province of current historiography, one realizes that it can be done only by challenging all rationalisms, whether great or small, so that this mass of imaginations can no longer be called either false or true. But then, if one succeeds in elaborating a doctrine that holds that beliefs can be neither true nor false, the result is that the supposedly rational domains, such as social and economic history, will in turn have to be seen as neither true nor false; they are not justified by a scheme that establishes their causes as a reason. This tactic of encirclement would ultimately lead us to abandon everything that has concerned us for several decades: human sciences, Marxism, and the sociology of knowledge.

Political history, for example, is most certainly not the history of twenty or fifty million French people; but for all its concern with events and rapidity, it is nevertheless not anecdotal. Eternal realities—government, domination, Power, the State—cannot explain the haze of detailed events. Such noble draperies are nothing but rationalist abstractions laid over programs whose diversity is secretly enormous. Eternal Politics has varied as much from the time of Louis XIV down to our own day as the economic realities; elucidating this program is what makes it possible to explain the debris of the treaties and battles and find an interest in them. The same could be said of literary history: to relate it to society is an undertaking that no one has accomplished and which is perhaps less false than hollow. The historicity of literary history is not there. It resides in the enormous unconscious changes that over three centuries have affected what we have not ceased to designate with the illusory terms "literature," "the beautiful," "taste," and "art." Not only have the relationships between "literature" and "society" changed; the Beautiful itself, Art itself, have been transformed. Indeed, the core of these realities contains nothing immutable to leave to the philosophers. They are historical, not philosophical. There is no core. And the forces and relations of production . . . ? Let us say that they determine the rest (this statement is less false than it is purely linguistic, the "rest" being itself an element of these forces and relations that determine it; but let that be). Production and its relationships are not just anything, and they are not self-evident. They are determined to a varying degree by the totality of history in its different moments. They are found in programs that still remain to be elucidated. This is a bit like the case of two closely related varieties of the same animal species, found in the same territory and endowed with the same resources, which have evolved to become as different as insectivores and carnivores. We were saying earlier that one sees no mode of conduct that is not arbitrary in its fashion; this amounts to saying that any mode of conduct is as irrational as any other. As Ramsay MacMullen recently wrote in *Past and Present* (1980), "Our concentration . . . on the irrational would involve a radical change in the nature of serious historiography."

Throughout this book we have tried to make our story tenable by confining ourselves to the irrationalist hypothesis. We have given no functional role to the impulse of reason, to natural understanding, or to a relationship between ideas and society. Our hypothesis can be stated in this way as well: At each moment, nothing exists or acts outside these palaces of the imagination (except the half-existence of "material" realities—that is, realities whose existence has not yet been accounted for and which has not received its form: fireworks or a military explosive, in the case of gunpowder).[215] These palaces are not built in space, then. They are the only space available. They project their own space when they arise. There is no repressed negativity around them that seeks to enter. Nothing exists, then, but

121

what the imagination, which has brought forth the palace, has constituted.

These sorts of clearings in the void are occupied by interests—social, economic, symbolic, or any other kind. The world that figures in our hypothesis will have the same ferocity as the one we know. These interests are not transhistorical. They are what they can be based on the possibilities offered by each palace. They are even the palace itself going by another name. If the polygon of causes now alters, the palace (which is the polygon going by yet another name) will be replaced by yet another palace that will constitute yet another space. This partial or total substitution might involve accounting for virtualities that had remained purely material up until then. But if such an accounting occurs, it will result from a happy convergence of circumstances and not be the product of an ongoing necessity. In short, not one of these palaces is the work of a champion of functional architecture. To put it another way, nothing will be more variable than the conception of rationality made by these successive architects, and nothing will be more immutable than the illusion by which each palace will pass for being adapted to reality. For each state of fact will be taken for the truth of things. The illusion of truth will make each palace appear to be completely situated inside the frontiers of reason.

Nothing equals the assurance and perseverance with which we ceaselessly open these broad extensions into the void. The opposition between truth and error is not on the scale of this phenomenon. It is a small thing. The opposition between reason and myth does not match it either. Myth is not an essence but a catchall, and reason is dissipated into a thousand little arbitrary rationalities.[216] Even the opposition between truth and fiction appears as secondary and historical; the distinction between the imaginary and the real no less so. Less absolute conceptions of truth as a simple regulating idea, the ideal of research, cannot be responsible for the amplitude acquired by our palaces of imagination, which have the spontaneity of natural productions and are probably neither true nor false. They are not functional, either, and not all of them are beautiful. They have at least one value, all too rarely mentioned, which we bring up only when we do not know quite what the interest of something is: they are interesting. For they are complicated.

Some of these palaces claim to be related to a model of practical truth and to embody the true politics, the true morality . . . If the model existed and the imitation had failed, they would be false. But if there is no model at all, they are no more false than true. Other palaces are doctrinal constructions that claim to reflect the truth of things. But if this supposed truth is only an arbitrary lighting that we shine on things, their program of truth is worth no more nor less than any other. Moreover, truth is the least of the issues among the doctrines that claim to assert a right to it. The most unbridled imaginings cannot deter them. Their profound impulse is not turned toward the true but toward amplitude. They arise from the same organizing capacity as the works of nature. A tree is neither true nor false; it is complicated.

These palaces of culture have no more utility to "society" than the living species comprising nature are useful to nature. What is called society is, moreover, nothing more than the rather unstructured group of these cultural palaces (it is in this way that a bourgeoisie can accommodate itself as easily to the company of the enlightened as to Puritan piety). It is an amorphous aggregate, but it proliferates. Mythical storytelling is a fine example of this proliferation of culture.

It is a proliferation that defies our rationalisms. We have to be accurate when we trim them of these shoots, which are as gratuitous as vegetation. The reductionism of mythmaking operates in several ways, each of them egocentric, for each epoch takes itself to be the center of culture.

The first way states that myth tells the truth. It is the allegorical mirror of eternal truths that are our own. Or else it is the slightly distorting mirror of past events, which either resemble today's political events (myth is historical) or are at the root of today's political individualities (myth is etiological). By reducing myth to history or *aitia,* the Greeks were led to make the world begin a little more than two millennia before themselves. First came a mythical prologue, followed by their historical past, which lasted for close to a millennium. For they never doubted for an instant that the most ancient humanity of memory was the first humanity to exist. The oldest known person is the founder. Neither would a noble of the French Old Regime think of being more precise when he noted the following in his family chronicle: "The founder of our race was Godron de Bussy, who in 931 gave a field to the abbey of Flavigny," for this donation was the oldest document that his charter contained.

However, some Greek thinkers were of the opinion that the world, including its human, animal, and divine fauna, was much older or had even existed for all eternity. How can this immensity be reduced to the scope of our reason? Their solution was to believe in a truth of things and a truth of man. The world in process is a perpetual beginning, for everything is periodically destroyed by catastrophes, and the mythical age is only the last of these periods. This is what Plato teaches in book 3 of the *Laws*. Throughout each one of these cycles the same realities and the same inventions reappear, like a cork that the nature of things ceaselessly lets bob to the surface of the most agitated waters. In book 7 of Aristotle's *Politics* we find an impressive example of this confidence in the natural truth: "For a long time," writes the philosopher, "political theory has recognized that, in the cities, the class of warriors must be distinct from that of the laborers." As for the institution of communal meals (where all citizens eat together every day, with the city offering the spectacle of a monastic refectory), it is no less ancient and has, as its authors, Minos in Crete and Italus in Italy. "However," adds Aristotle, "it is better to think that these institutions, like many others, were invented a great number of times throughout the ages or, rather, an infinite number of times." These last words are to be taken literally. Aristotle believes in the eternity of the world and, consequently, in the myth of the Eternal Return. He does not envision it as the dealing of different hands in a kind of cosmic poker game in which the inevitable return of the same aggregates would, far from having a reason, confirm that everything is combined by chance alone (and not through a causal scheme). He sees it in a more reassuring way, as a cyclical tide of the same realities that the truth of things enables one to discover; it is a happy ending.

We moderns no longer believe in the cycle but in evolution. For a long time humanity was a youngster; now it has grown up and does not tell itself any more myths. It has left behind, or is going to emerge from, its prehistory. Our philosophy always has the mission of reassuring and blessing, but it is the (r)evolution that now must be comforted. In our eyes myth has ceased to tell the truth. On the other hand, it passes for having spoken for something. Lacking a truth, it had a social or vital function. Truth itself egocentrically remains our own. The social function filled by myth confirms that we are in the truth of things when we explain evolution by society. The same could be said of the function of ideology, and this is why this last term is so dear to us. All of that is very good, but here is the catch: what if there is no truth of things?

When a city, or indeed a palace, is put in the middle of the desert, the palace is no more true or false than the rivers or the mountains, which lack a model mountain to follow. The palace simply is, and with it emerges an order of things about which something can be said. The inhabitants of the palace will find that this arbitrary order conforms with the very *truth of things*, for this superstition helps them to live; but some historians or philosophers among them will confine themselves to trying to *speak truthfully* about the palace and recall that it could not conform to a model that has no existence. Or, to change metaphors, nothing shines in the night of the world. The materiality of things has no natural phosphorescence, and no luminous beacon indicates the route to take, either. Men cannot learn anything, since there still isn't anything to learn. But the accidents of human history, as erratic and unplanned as the successive hands in a poker game, lead men to shine an endlessly changeable lighting on their affairs. Only then is the materiality of things reflected in any light. This lighting is no more true or false than any other, but it begins to make a certain world exist. It is a spontaneous creation, the product of an imagination. When a lighted clearing appears in this way, it is generally taken for the very truth, since there is nothing else to see. Similarly, one can make statements that are true or false concerning what the lighting reveals at each point. These are products of the imagination, for the successive lightings cannot conform to a materiality that in our eyes does not exist independently of the lighting that reveals it, and their succession cannot be explained by the dialectical exigencies of a vocation for rationality, either. The world has promised us nothing, and we cannot read our truths in it.

The idea that it is impossible to rely on the authority of the truth is what distinguishes modern philosophy from its counterfeits. Yes, imagination is fashionable; irrationalism is more in vogue than reason (it means that nothing else is truly reasonable), and the unsaid improvises. But this is the point: does this unsaid merely exist, or is it a good thing that must be allowed to speak (or, what amounts to the same thing, something bad that must not be allowed to speak, for there is a truth, the civilizing force of self-discipline)? Does it resemble nature (or, what amounts to the same thing, a continually reappearing barbarism)? Cast out into whatever void surrounds the current palace, does it inevitably seek readmittance? Should we open the door to it? Do things have inscribed in them a natural tendency, which is our vocation, so that, if we follow it, we are good people? Here we have some very old wines named reason, morality, God, and truth, poured into new bottles. These wines seem to have a modern flavor if they are put into bottles known as demystification, the undermining of consciousness and language, philosophy as an upside-down world, or the criticism of ideologies. Except that these bitter and dramatic novels end happily, like those of the old days. We have been promised a happy ending. There is a path, which is reassuring, and this path is our career, which is exciting. Fraud is easily recognized by the human warmth it exudes. Above all, do not give me fervor, Nathanael. It would be demagoguery to imply that the reflective analysis of a program or a "discourse" results in the inauguration of a truer program or the supplanting of bourgeois society with one that is more just. Such analysis can lead only to another society, another program or discourse. It is perfectly permissible to prefer this new society or this new truth; one need only refrain from calling it more true or more just.

We do not claim, then, that prudence is the true way and that one only has to stop deifying history and fight the good fight against the ideologies that have done so much harm. This program of conservatism is as arbitrary as any other. If we take numbers of millions of dead as our measure, patriotism, which no one talks about any more, has created and will go on creating as many victims as the ideologies that exclusively rouse our indignation. So what is to be done? That, precisely, is the question we should not ask. To be against fascism and communism—or patriotism—is one thing. All living beings live on opinions, and those of my dog are to be against hunger, thirst, and the mailman and to ask to play ball. Nevertheless, he does not wonder what he ought to do and what he is permitted to hope. We want philosophy to answer these questions, and we judge it on its answers; but only a blatant anthropocentrism will assume that a problem contains its solution simply because we need one and that philosophies that give reasons for living are more true than the others. Moreover, these questions are less natural than we may think. They do not simply present themselves. Most times have not exhibited self-doubt and have not asked such questions. For what is called philosophy has served as a booth that exhibits the most varied of interrogative wares. What is the world? How can one be happy, i.e., autarchic? How do we make our questions conform to the revealed wisdom? What is the path to self-transfiguration? How does one organize society to move with the flow of history? The questions are forgotten before the answers are found.

Historical reflection is a criticism that diminishes the pretensions of knowledge and is limited to speaking truly about truths without presuming that a true Politics or Science exists. Is this criticism contradictory, and can one say that it is true that there are no truths? Yes, and by this we are not playing the game, taken from the Greeks, of the liar who is lying when he says, "I lie"—which therefore is the truth. One is a liar not in general but in particular when one says this or that. An individual who would say, "I have always made up stories," would not be making up a tale in saying that if he specified, "My storytelling consisted in believing that my successive imaginations were truths inscribed on the nature of things."

For if my current truth of man and things were true, universal culture would be false, and it still would be necessary to explain this reign of falsehood and my exclusive access to truth. Would we be seeking the kernel of truth within falsehood in the manner of the Greeks? Would we be giving mythmaking a vital function, as Bergson did, or a social one, as the sociologists have done? The only way for us to get out of this quandary is to posit that culture, without being false, is not true, either. I have gone to Descartes for that—he who wrote in letters to his friends, not daring to put it in print, that God had created not only things but also truths, so that two and two would not make four if He had so wished it. For God did not create what was already true; the only things that were true were what he had created as true, and the true and the false existed only after he had created them. It is enough to give this divine constitutive power, this power to create without the need for a preexisting model, to man's constitutive imagination.

At first, thinking that nothing is either true or false has an odd effect, but one quickly gets used to it. And with good reason: the value of the truth is useless, it is always double-sided. Truth is the name we give to the choices to which we cling. If we let go of them, we would emphatically say they were false, for we respect the truth so much. Even the Nazis respected it. They said that they were right; they did not say that they were wrong. We could have answered them that they were mistaken, but what was the point? They were not on the same wavelength as we were, and it is platonic to accuse an earthquake of being false.

Must we exclaim that the human condition is tragic and unhappy if men do not have the right to believe in what they do and if they are doomed to see themselves the same way as they see their ancestors, who believed in Zeus and Heracles? This misfortune is not real. It is on paper, a rhetorical theme. It could exist only because of reflectivity, which only historians cultivate. Now, historians are not unhappy; they are interested. As for other men, reflectivity does not stifle them or paralyze their interests. Furthermore, the programs of truth remain implicit, unknown to those who practice them and who call what they adhere to the truth. The idea of truth appears only when one takes the other person into account. It is not primary; it reveals a secret weakness. How does it happen that the truth is so little true? Truth is the thin layer of gregarious self-satisfaction that separates us from the will to power.

Only historical reflection can clarify the programs of truth and reveal their variations. But this reflection is not a constant beacon and does not mark a stage on the route taken by humanity. The road twists and turns. The truth does not direct it toward the horizon. Nor are its vagaries molded on the powerful contours of an infrastructure. The road winds haphazardly. Most of the time the travelers do not care. Each one believes that his road is the true one, and the turns that he sees others take scarcely disturb him. But on rare occasions it happens that a bend in the road permits the travelers to look back and see a long stretch of the road and all its zigzags. Some travelers are of such a temperament that this sight moves them. This retrospective vision speaks truly, but it does not make the road any more false, since the road could not be true. Therefore, the flashes of retrospective lucidity are not very important. They are simple accidents of the journey; they do not permit one to find the straight road, nor do they mark a stage in the trip. They do not even transform the individuals that they touch. We do not find that historians are more disinterested than the common run of mortals or that they vote any differently, since man is not a thinking reed. Could this be because I wrote this book in the country? I was envying the placidity of the animals.

The theme of this book was very simple. Merely by reading the title, anyone with the slightest historical background would immediately have answered, "But of course they believed in their myths!" We have simply wanted also to make it clear that what is true of "them" is also true of ourselves and to bring out the implications of this primary truth.

Notes

Introduction

1. Beneath the earth the dead continue to lead the life they had led while living. In Hell, Minos continues to judge, just as Orion continues to hunt below the earth (M. Nilsson, *Geschichte der griechischen Religion*, 2d ed. [Munich: Beck, 1955], vol. 1, p. 677). It should not be said, as Racine did, that the gods made Minos the judge of the dead. On the highly conscious lies of the poets, see Plutarch, *Quomodo adulescens poetas* 2.16F–17F.

2. Plutarch, *Life of Theseus* 15.2–16.2. Cf. W. Den Boet, "Theseus, the Growth of a Myth in History," *Greece and Rome* 16 (1969): 1–13.

3. Plutarch, *Life of Theseus* 1.5: "*mythōdes* purified by *logos.*" The opposition between *logos* and *mythos* comes from Plato, *Gorgias* 523A.

4. Thucydides 1.4.1: "to know by hearsay" is to know by myth. Compare, for example, Pausanias 8.10.2. Herodotus (3.122) had the same idea about Minos. Cf. Aristotle, *Politics* 1271b38.

5. W. Nestle, *Vom Mythos zum Logos* (Stuttgart: Metzler, 1940). Another important book for the different questions we are examining here is that by John Forsdyke, *Greece before Homer: Ancient Chronology and Mythology* (New York, 1957).

6. A. Rostagni, *Poeti alessandrini*, new ed. (Rome: Bretschneider, 1972), pp. 148, 264. As proof, the historical or naturalist exegesis of myths by Thucydides or Ephorus, the allegorical exegesis of the Stoics and rhetoricians, euhemerism, and the novelistic stylization of myths by the Hellenistic poets.

7. Cited by G. Couton in an important study, "Les *Pensées* de Pascal contre la thèse des trois imposteurs," *XVIIᵉ Siècle* 32 (1980): 183.

8. As Renan more or less said, all that is needed in order to no longer be able to prove the nonexistence of a miracle is to admit the existence of the supernatural. It is enough to have an interest in believing that Auschwitz did not take place for the eyewitness accounts of Auschwitz to become unbelievable. Nor has anyone ever proved that Zeus did not exist. See the examples in notes 11 and 27.

9. G. Huppert, *L'idée de l'histoire parfaite* (Paris: Flammarion, 1973), p. 7.

10. Quoted by Huppert, p. 7, n. 1. The various essays of A. D. Momigliano that relate to these problems of history and the method of historiography can now be conveniently found in his two collections: *Studies in Historiography* (London: Weidenfeld & Nicholson, 1966) and *Essays in Ancient and Modern Historiography* (Oxford: Blackwell, 1977).

11. If one wishes to see the degree of futility of "rigor," "method," and "criticism of sources" in these realms, we need only quote the lines with which, as late as 1838, V. Leclerc intends to refute Niebuhr: "To proscribe the history of a time because fables have had a part in it is to proscribe the history of all times. The first centuries of Rome are suspect to us because of the she-wolf of Romulus, the shields of Numa, the appearance of Castor and Pollux. Then erase from Roman history the whole story of Caesar because of the star that appeared at his death, and that of Augustus, since he was said to be the son of Apollo disguised as a snake" (*Des journaux chez les Romains* [Paris, 1838], p. 166). Hence we see that the skepticism of Beaufort and Niebuhr is based not on the distinction between primary and secondary sources but on the biblical criticism of the thinkers of the eighteenth century.

12. Earlier scholars have speculated that Pausanias did most of his traveling in books. It can be stated that this is incorrect. Pausanias worked above all on-site. See the very lively passage by Ernst Meyer in his abridged translation of Pausanias: *Pausanias, Beschreibung Griechenlands*, 2d ed. (Munich and Zurich: Artemis Verlag, 1967), Introduction, p. 42. See also K. E. Müller, *Geschichte der antiken Ethnographie* (Wiesbaden: Steiner, 1980), vol. 2, pp. 176–80.

1. When Historical Truth Was Tradition and Vulgate

13. Formulas such as "the people of the region say that . . ." or "the Thebans tell that . . ." could very well, in the case of Pausanias, refer to what we would call a written source. Except that, in Pausanias' eyes, this writing is not a source; tradition, obviously oral, is the source, of which this is only the transcription. In his research on Arcadia (8.10.2), Pausanias declares, for example, "I learned that by *akoē*, by hearsay, and all my predecessors as well." Similarly, it is by *akoē* that the story of Tiresias is known (9.33.2). This means that Pausanias and his predecessors (whom we would regard as Pausanias' sources) did not observe the matter with their own eyes (see 9.39.14), but only transcribed what oral tradition said. As we see, Pausanias ably distinguishes the primary source (*akoē*) from the secondary. We know who his predecessors are: at the beginning of his Arcadian researches, Pausanias mentions, in passing and only once, an epic poet, Asius, whom he had read a great deal and whom he cites fairly often elsewhere (8.1.4: "Asius has some verses on this subject"; seven lines further back, Pausanias had written, "The Arcadians say that . . ."). We would say that Asius reproduces Arcadian traditions. For Pausanias, the only true source is contemporaneous evidence, given by those who were there. Thus it is an irreparable loss if these contemporaries fail to transmit in writing what they have seen (1.6.1; cf. Flavius Josephus, *The Jewish Wars* 1.5.15). Historians only reproduce this source, whether in oral or written form. They are continually establishing the correct version of the event. This state of affairs is so taken for granted that they cite their source only if they diverge from it (thus Pausanias [1.9.8] cites Hieronymus of Cardia only when he differs from him on some detail). Truth is anonymous, only error is personal. In some societies this principle is taken very far indeed; cf. Renan's remarks on the formation of the Pentateuch (*Oeuvres complètes*, vol. 6, p. 520): "High antiquity did not have the idea of the authenticity of the book. Everyone wanted his own copy to be complete and made all the necessary additions to keep it up to date. At that time a text was not recopied; it was redone by combining it with other documents. Every book was composed with

absolute objectivity, without a title or the author's name, ceaselessly transformed and undergoing endless additions.'' Today, in India, popular editions are published of the Upanishads, which are one or two thousand years old but which are naïvely completed in order to be true; e.g., mention of the discovery of electricity is sometimes made. Falsification is not the issue; by completing or correcting a book that, like the telephone directory, is simply true, one is not falsifying it. In other words, what is at stake here is not the notion of truth but that the notion of author. See also H. Peter, *Wahrheit und Kunst: Geschichtschreigung und Plagiat im klass. Altertum* (1911; reprinted, Hildesheim: G. Olms, 1965), p. 436. On historical knowledge by hearsay, see now F. Hartog, *Le Miroir d'Hérodote: Essai sur la représentation de l'autre* (Paris: Gallimard, 1981), pp. 272 ff.

14. Not all of the informants (''exegetes'') that Pausanias mentions a score of times were our author's *ciceroni*, for he also designates his written sources as ''exegetes'' (Ernst Meyer, p. 37, citing 1.42.4). On these exegetes, see also W. Kroll, *Studien zum Verständnis der römischen Literatur* (Stuttgart: Metzler, 1924), p. 313. See also note 159, below.

15. Huppert, *L'idée de l'histoire parfaite*, p. 36.

16. Thucydides 1.20–22.

17. Momigliano, *Studies in Historiography*, p. 214.

18. Thucydides 1.20.2.

19. Pausanias 8.8.3; Herodotus 7.152.3. Cf. Kurt Latte, ''Histoire et Historiens de l'Antiquité,'' p. 11 (in *Entretiens sur l'Antiquité classique, Fondation Hardt* 4, 1956); in 3.9.2 Herodotus gives two versions, not believing for a moment in the second, but ''he speaks of it anyway, since it is spoken of.'' What ''is said'' has already taken on a kind of existence.

20. Momigliano, *Essays in Ancient and Modern Historiography*, p. 145; *Studies in Historiography*, p. 217.

21. See note 13 for this expression of Renan's. As everyone knows, the strange texts cited in the *Augustan History* are fakes, but it is an imitation of the taste shared by Hellenistic and Roman antiquity for all sorts of collections of curiosities. Suetonius and Diogenes Laertius likewise quote letters from Augustus and the philosophers' testaments, not to establish facts but as curious and rare pieces. Here the document is an end in itself and not a means; these authors draw no conclusion or argument from the pieces they quote, which are not at all ''relevant documents.'' On Porphyry's use of citation in his *De Abstinentia*, see W. Pötscher, *Theophrastos, Peri Eusebeias* (Leiden: Brill, 1964), pp. 12 and 120; cf. Diodorus 2.55–60, citing or transcribing Iamboulos. Cf. also P. Hadot, *Porphyre et Victorinus* (Paris: Etudes Augustiniennes, 1968), vol. 1, p. 33.

22. Pausanias 1.3.3.

23. No more than Thucydides did (2.15). Indeed, Aristotle does not doubt the historicity of Theseus; he sees in him the founder of Athenian democracy (*Constitution of Athens* 41.2) and reduces to verisimilitude the myth of the Athenian children deported to Crete and delivered to the Minotaur (*Constitution of the Bottiaeans*, cited by Plutarch, *Life of Theseus* 16.2). As for the Minotaur, more than four centuries before Pausanias the historian Philochorus also reduced him to verisimilitude; he claimed to have found a tradition (he does not specify whether it is oral or transcribed) among the Cretans

according to which these children were not devoured by the Minotaur but were given as prizes to the victors in a gymnastic competition; this contest was won by a cruel and very vigorous man named Taurus (cited by Plutarch 16.1). Since this Taurus commanded the army of Minos, he was really the Taurus of Minos: Minotaur.

24. Herodotus 3.122: "Polycrates was the first Greek we know of to plan the dominion of the sea, unless we count Minos of Cnossus and any other who may possibly have ruled the sea at a still earlier date. In ordinary human history, at any rate, Polycrates was the first." As early as the *Iliad*, what has been called Homeric rationalism limits the intervention of the gods in human affairs to mythical times.

25. Pausanias 8.8.3. For the Greeks, myth in itself posed no problem; there was only the problem of the unlikely elements it contained. This criticism of myth begins with Hecataeus of Miletus (who already was making fun of the ridiculous things the Hellenes were saying [fr. 1, Jacoby]); cf., in Pausanias 3.25.5, the criticism of the myth of Cerberus by Hecataeus.

26. H. Hitzig, "Zur Pausaniasfrage," in *Festschrift des philologischen Kränzchens in Zürich zu der in Zürich im Herbst 1887 tagenden 39, Versammlung deutscher Philolgen und Schulmänner*, p. 57.

27. Here is an example: Newton states that the seven kings of Rome reigned for a total of two hundred forty-four years and notices that an equally long period of reigns is without par in universal history, where the average length of a reign is seventeen years. He could have concluded from this that the chronology of royal Rome was legendary; he concluded instead that it was false, reduced it to seven times seventeen years, and thus set the date of the foundation of Rome at 630 B.C. See Isaac Newton, *The Chronology of Ancient Kingdoms* (French trans., 1728).

2. The Plurality and Analogy of True Worlds

28. M. Nilsson, *Geschichte der griech. Religion*, 2d ed., vol. 1, pp. 14 and 371; A. D. Nock, *Essays on Religion and the Ancient World* (Oxford: Clarendon Press, 1972), vol. 1, p. 261. I am not even sure that it is necessary to make an exception for etiological myths. Very few Greek myths explain rites, and those that do are less the invention of priests, wishing to lay the foundations for a rite, than the imaginings of ingenious local minds, who fabricated a fanciful explanation for whatever cultural peculiarity intrigued the traveler. Myth explains rite, but this rite is only a local curiosity. Varro's Stoic distinction of three categories of gods is still fundamental: the gods of the city, to whom men made cult; the gods of the poets, that is, those of mythology; and the gods of the philosophers (P. Boyancé, *Etudes sur la religion romaine* [Ecole française de Rome, 1972], p. 254). On the relationship between myth, sovereignty, and genealogy in the archaic period, see J.-P. Vernant, who has reopened the question in *Les Origines de la pensée grecque* (Paris: Presses Universitaires de France, 1962) and *Mythe et pensée chez les Grecs* (Paris: Maspero, 1965), and see also M. I. Finley, "Myth, Memory, and History," *History and Theory* 4 (1965): 281–302. We are dealing with this attitude toward myth, since our subject is its transformation during the Greco-Roman period, but we state our agreement with the doctrine of the historicity of reason as presented by J.-P. Vernant in *Religions, Histoires, Raisons* (Paris: Payot, 1979), p. 97.

29. For one example among a myriad of others, but a lovely one, see Pausanias 7.23; on local scholars, see W. Kroll, *Studien zum Verständnis*, p. 308.

30. A. van Gennep, *Religions, Moeurs et Légendes* (Paris, 1911), vol. 3, p. 150; E. Mâle, *L'Art religieux du XIII^{e}siècle en France* (Paris: Armand Colin, 1948), p. 269; E. Mâle, *L'Art religieux de la fin du XVI^{e}siècle* (Paris: Armand Colin, 1951), p. 132.

31. Cf. Veyne, *Le Pain et Le Cirque* (Paris: Seuil, 1976), p. 589.

32. Saint Augustine does not question the historicity of Aeneas, but, since myth is reduced to verisimilitude, Aeneas is no more the son of Venus than Romulus is the son of Mars (*City of God* 1.4 and 3.2–6). We will see that Cicero, Livy, and Dionysius of Halicarnassus did not believe in the divine birth of Romulus, either.

33. The plurality of the modalities of belief is too much a commonplace for it to be necessary for us to dwell on it; see J. Piaget, *La Formation du symbole chez l'enfant* (Paris: Delachaux & Niestlé, 1939), p. 177; Alfred Schutz, *Collected Papers* (The Hague: Nijhoff, coll. "Phaenomenologica," 1960–66), vol. 1, p. 232: "On Multiple Realities"; vol. 2, p. 135: "Don Quixote and the Problem of Reality"; Pierre Janet, *De l'angoisse à l'extase* (Paris: Alcan, 1926), vol. 1, p. 244. It is no less a commonplace that one believes different truths concerning the same object simultaneously; children know both that toys are brought by Santa Claus and that they are given to them by their parents. J. Piaget, *Le Jugement et le raisonnement chez l'enfant* (Paris: Delachaux & Niestlé, 1945), p. 217; cf. p. 325: "For the child there are several heterogeneous realities: play, observable reality, the world of things that are heard and said, etc.; these realities are more or less incoherent and independent. As a result, when the child goes from the state of work to the state of play, or the state of submission to adult authority to that of self-examination, his opinions can vary strikingly." M. Nilsson, *Geschichte der griech. Religion*, vol. 1, p. 50: "A child of thirteen years, bathing in a stream ruffled by a thousand tiny waves, says, 'The stream is frowning'; if such an expression were taken literally, this would be a myth; but at the same time the child knows that the stream was made of water, that one may drink there, etc. In the same way, a primitive can see souls everywhere in nature, he can place in a tree a sentient and active force that he must appease or honor; but at another time he will still chop this tree down to obtain materials for building or burning." See also Max Weber, *Wirtschaft und Gesellschaft* (Tübingen: Mohr, 1976), vol. 1, p. 245. Wolfgang Leonard, *Die Revolution entlässt ihre Kinder* (Frankfurt: Ullstein Bücher, 1955), p. 58 (the author was nineteen and a komsomol at the time of Stalin's great purge in 1937): "My mother had been arrested, I had been present at the arrest of my professors and my friends, and of course I had noticed a long time ago that Soviet reality did not at all resemble the way it was represented in *Pravda*. But in some way I separated these things, as well as my personal expressions and experiences, from my political convictions based on principle. It was almost as if there were two planes: that of daily events or my own experience (in which it was not unusual for me to display a critical spirit) and another one, that of the General Party Line, which I was continuing, despite a certain uneasiness, to hold as right, 'at least fundamentally.' I believe that many komsomols know such a dichotomy." Thus, it does not at all seem that myth has been taken as history or that the difference between legend and history has been abolished, despite E. Köhler, *L'Aventure chevaleresque: Idéal et réalité dans le monde courtois* (Paris: Gallimard, 1971), p. 8. Rather, let us say that children can

believe in myth as much as in history but not instead of it or under the same conditions; nor do children require their parents to display the gifts of levitation, ubiquity, and invisibility that they attribute to Santa Claus. Children, primitives, and believers of all kinds are not naïve. "Even primitives do not confuse an imaginary relationship with a real one" (Evans-Pritchard, *Primitive Religion,* Fr. trans. [Paris: Payot, coll. "Petite Bibliothèque Payot," n.d.], p. 49). "The symbolism of the Huichol admits the identity between the wheat and the stag. Lévy-Bruhl does not want us to speak of symbols here, but rather of prelogical thought. But the logic of the Huichol would be prelogical only on the day that he made a gruel of wheat while believing he was making venison stew" (Olivier Leroy, *La Raison primitive* [Paris: Geuthner, 1927], p. 70). "The Sedang Moï of Indochina, who have established a way to enable man to give up his human status and become a boar, nonetheless react differently according to whether they are dealing with a true boar or a nominal one" (G. Deveureux, *Ethnopsychanalyse complémentariste* [Paris: Flammarion, 1972], p. 101). "In spite of verbal traditions, people rarely take a myth in the same sense that they take an empirical truth; all the doctrines that have flourished in the world on the subject of the immortality of the soul have hardly affected man's natural feeling when confronted with death" (G. Santayana, *The Life of Reason,* vol. 3: *Reason in Religion* [New York, 1905], p. 52). Many are the ways of believing, or, to put it more accurately, many are the registers of truth of a single object.

34. Hermann Fränkel, *Wege und Formen frühgriech. Denkens,* 2d ed. (Munich: Beck, 1960), p. 366. By telling him of the fine world of the heroes, Pindar honors the victor more than he would if he were merely praising him; being received by the Guermantes is more flattering than receiving their compliments. Therefore, says Fränkel, "The image of the victor is often more vague than that of the heroes." Because of this must we say, with Fränkel (*Dichtung und philosophie des frühen Griechentums* [Munich: Beck, 1962], p. 557), that this heroic and divine world is a "world of values"? But we can hardly say that the gods and heroes are saints; they honor *the* values the way distinguished mortals do themselves—neither more nor less. Here again, let us not fail to recognize mythological "snobbery." The heroes' world *has* value; it is more elevated than that of mortals. In the same fashion, for Proust a duchess is higher than a bourgeoise, but not because she cultivates all the values and virtues; it is because she is a duchess. Of course, as a duchess and because she is a duchess, she will have moral distinction and will cultivate these values, but this is a consequence. It is by its essence and not because of its merits that the heroic world has more value than the mortal world. If one were to judge that the word "snobbery," even used *cum grano salis,* is too strong for Pindar and his victors, one has only to reread an amusing passage from Plato's *Lysis* 205C–D, which deserves to be set as an epigraph in every edition of Pindar.

35. It is still the case in the *Aeneid* 1.8: "Musa, mihi causas memora." By this Hellenizing expression, Virgil asks the Muse to "repeat" to him and guarantee what "is said" on the subject of Aeneas. He is not asking the Muse to "remind" him of something he would have forgotten or not known. It is for this reason, one would believe, that the Muses are the daughters of Memoria (*contra* Nilsson, *Geschichte der griech. Religion,* vol. 1, p. 254).

36. W. Kroll, *Studien zum Verständnis,* pp. 49–58. Lines 27 and 28 of Hesiod's *Theogony* are not simple; the Muses inspire lies, but also truths. Posterity will often understand that poets mix all the truths with lies or add lies to truths (cf. Strabo 1.2.9. C.

20 on Homer). Others will see here the opposition between the epic, which lies, and didactic poetry, which tells the truth. It is undoubtedly better to understand that, without presenting himself as a "didactic" poet, Hesiod opposes his own version of the divine and human genealogies to those of Homer, whom he takes as his rival and predecessor.

37. On this historiography, see, for example, J. Forsdyke, quoted above, n. 5; M. Nilsson, *Geschichte der griech. Religion,* 2d ed., vol. 2, pp. 51–54.

38. See Pausanias 4.6.1 for Myron; for Rhianus, read 4.1–24 *passim.* On this Rhianus, see A. Lesky, *Geschichte der griech. Literatur* (Bern and Munich: Francke, 1963), p. 788; I have not read *Pausanias und Rhianos* by J. Kroymann (Berlin, 1943) nor the *Messenische Studien* by F. Kiechle (Kallmünz, 1959). On Pausanias' sources for Arcadian archeology, see W. Nestle, *Vom Mythos zum Logos,* pp. 145 ff. On the notions of beginning, establishment (*katastasis*), and "archeology," see E. Norden, *Agnostos Theos* (Darmstadt: Wiss. Buchg., 1956), p. 372.

39. Pausanias 8.6.1. But we would have to quote the entire beginning of the eighth book. For the founding of Oenotria, see 8.3.5.

40. Whatever one says, the most widespread conceptions of time view it as neither cyclical or linear but as decline (Lucretius takes it as obvious); everything is made and invented; the world is adult and therefore has only to age; cf. Veyne, *Comment on écrit l'histoire,* p. 57, note 4 of the paperback edition (Paris: Seuil, 1979). This conception is the implicit key to a difficult sentence in Plato, *Laws* 677C, for whom there would no longer be any place for inventions (which are only reinventions) if the great majority of humanity were not periodically destroyed, along with all its cultural acquisitions.

41. Polybius 10.21 (on the foundations of cities); 12.26D (Timaeus' boasting about the foundations and about kinships among cities); 38.6 (historical accounts limited to telling origins, thus saying nothing about the rest of the history). Popular thought opposed the past of "foundations" to the monotonous present; the first was enchanting. When Hippias went to give lectures in Sparta, he spoke "of heroic, or human genealogies, of the foundation of cities in primitive times, more generally, of what pertained to ancient days" (Plato, *Hippias Major* 285E). This founding of the established (and even declining) world that is ours comprises three elements: "the foundation of towns, the invention of the arts, and the writing of the laws" (Josephus, *Contra Apion* 1.2.7). Herodotus travels the world, describes every people as one would describe a house, and proceeds to the basement, i.e., the origin of this people.

42. Examples of all these facts can be found throughout Pausanias, particularly in the opening chapters of the various books. Explaining a toponym by an anthroponym permits one to return to human origins, so it was preferable to explain a mountain called Nomia by using the name of a nymph instead of with the word that means "pasturelands," which would obviously be the good explanation, as Pausanias himself hints (8.38.11); Pausanias also wanted to explain the name of Aigialeus by the word *aigialos,* "shore," but the Achaeans preferred to invent a king named Aigialeus for an explanation (8.1.1).

43. Pausanias 8.1.4; likewise, in Thucydides 1.3: "Hellen and his sons" are no longer the fathers of all the Hellenes, nor their mythical prototypes, as the Elephant is for all the elephants. They represent a royal dynasty that reigned over a human society. For an example of historical etiology, see Aristophanes' parody in *The Birds* 466–546.

3. The Social Distribution of Knowledge and Modalities of Belief

44. On the possession and distribution of the true, see the very fine book by Marcel Detienne, *Les Maîtres de vérité dans la Grèce archaïque* (Paris: Maspero, 1967); on the distribution of knowledge, see Alfred Schutz, *Collected Papers* (Coll. "Phaenomenologica," vols. 11 and 15), vol. 1, p. 14: "The Social Distribution of Knowledge," and vol. 2, p. 120: "The Well-Informed Citizen"; G. Deleuze, *Différence et Répétition* (Paris: Presses Universitaires de France, 1968), p. 203. Christian thinkers, particularly Saint Augustine, were led to mine the following idea: Is not the Church a society of belief? Saint Augustine's *De utilitate credendi* explains that we believe the word of others above all, that there is an exchange of unequally distributed information, and also that, by forcing people to believe, they end up really believing; this is the basis of the duty to persecute and of the sadly famous *compelle intrare*. Good must be done for people in spite of themselves (inequities of knowledge and power go together), and knowledge is a good. This sociology of faith could already be found in Origen, *Contra Celsum* 1.9–10 and 3.38. Out of this will emerge the doctrine of implicit faith: whoever trusts the Church will be deemed to know everything that it professes. Problem: Beginning with what degree of ignorance is a faithful Christian to be judged a Christian in name only? Does a person have faith if the only article of faith he knows is that the Church knows and is right? Cf. B. Groethuysen, *Origines de l'esprit bourgeois en France: l'Eglise et la bourgeoisie* (Paris: Gallimard, 1952), p. 12. On all the above, and on Saint Augustine, cf. Leibniz, *Nouveaux Essais*, vol. 4, p. 20. In addition to the political and social consequences, the distribution of knowledge has effects on knowledge itself (people learn and invent only if they have the socially recognized right to do so; otherwise they hesitate and doubt themselves). When people have no right to know and question, their ignorance and blindness are genuine. Therefore, Proust used to say, "Never confess." The very sources and proofs of knowledge are historical. For example, "If the Greek idea of truth is that of a proposition that is true because it is noncontradictory and verifiable, the Judeo-Christian idea of truth concerns sincerity, the absence of fraud or duplicity in personal relations" (R. Mehl, *Traité de sociologie du protestantisme* [Paris and Neuchâtel: Delachaux & Niestlé, 1966], p. 76). Whence, I suppose, the strange ending of the Fourth Gospel, where the group of the disciples of Saint John declares, "We know that his testimony is true" (21:24). If that was a testimony in the Greek sense of the word (the witness was there and saw the thing with his eyes), the phrase would be absurd, for how could they testify to the truth of the account that Saint John made of the death of Christ when they were not there? But the disciples mean that they knew John well and recognized a sincere heart incapable of lying.

45. This idea, the importance of which is well known for Saint Augustine, particularly in *De utilitate credendi*, can also be found in Galen, *De optima secta, ad Thrasybulum* 15.

46. Plato, *Phaedo* 85C and 99C–D.

47. Aristophanes, *Peace* 832; cf. *The Birds* 471 ff.

48. Nietzsche, *Aurora*, § 547: "Today, the march of science is no longer hindered by the accidental fact that man lives for about seventy years, but such was the case for a long time. . . . In olden days everyone wished to achieve full knowledge during this period of time, and the methods of learning were appreciated as a function of this

general desire. . . . Since the entire universe was organized around man, it was believed that the possibility of knowing things was likewise adapted to the scale of human life. . . . To resolve everything at once, in a single word, such was the secret desire; this task was imagined as having the aspect of a Gordian knot or the Dove's egg. One did not doubt that it was possible . . . to liquidate all questions with a single answer: it was an enigma that had to be solved.''

49. Plato, *Lysis* 205C–D.

50. Xenophanes, fragment 1.

51. Aristophanes, *The Wasps* 1179; Herodotus 1.60.

52. G. Le Bras, *Etudes de sociologie religieuse* (Paris: Presses Universitaires de France, 1955), pp. 60, 62, 68, 75, 112, 199, 240, 249, 267, 564, 583. This docile relationship within the field of knowledge (the symbolic field, in Bourdieu's terms) seems to us to be at least as important as the ideological content of religion, which is easier to see and easier to relate to social interests but also more equivocal. For Proudhon, Catholic cult taught respect for the social hierarchy, since at Mass and everywhere that priority and precedence are stressed, the proceedings emphasize social hierarchy; undoubtedly so, but in Voltaire's *Dictionnaire philosophique* (s.v. ''Idols'') there is a sentence, anti-Christian by the author's intent, that remains odd nonetheless: ''A rough and superstitious populace . . . that flocked to the temples out of idleness and because there the small are equal to the great.''

53. Aristophanes, *The Knights* 32; cf. Nilsson, *Geschichte der griech. Religion*, vol. 1, p. 780.

54. Polybius 6.56; for Flavius Josephus, Moses saw in religion a way to make virtue be respected (*Contra Apion* 2.160). The same utilitarian link between religion and morals is found in Plato, *Laws* 839C and 838B–D, and also in Aristotle, *Metaphysics* 1074b4.

55. Herodotus 2.42–45, quoted by M. Untersteiner, *La Fisiologia del mito*, 2d ed. (Florence: La Nuova Italia, 1972), p. 262.

4. Social Diversity of Beliefs and Mental Balkanization

56. Philostratus, *Imagines* 1.14(15), *Ariadne*. The theme of the nurse or mother who tells fables goes back to Plato (*Republic* 378C and *Laws* 887D). Nurses told frightening stories about Lamias and the Horses of the Sun, writes Tertullian (*Ad Valentinianus* 3). For Plato these are old wives' tales (*Lysis* 205D); these are the *aniles fabulae* of which Minucius Felix speaks (20.4), which we take from our *imperiti parentes* (24.1). In the *Heroicus* of Philostratus, the wine-grower asks the author: ''When did you begin to find myths unbelievable?'' and Philostratus, or his spokesperson, answers, ''A long time ago, when I was an adolescent; for while I was a child, I believed in such fables, and my nurse entertained me with these tales, which she accompanied with a pretty song; some of them even used to make her cry. But once I became a young man, I thought that these fables must not be lightly accepted'' (*Heroicus* 136–37 Kayser; p. 8, 3 De Lannoy). Quintilian also speaks of *aniles fabulae* (*Institutio oratoria* 1.8.19). In Euripides' *Hippolytus* (line 451) the nurse implicates the Learned in the affair. Before telling the fable of Semele, she cites the learned who have seen books on this legend. In a remarkable metric epitaph from Chios (Kaibel, *Epigrammata* 232), two old women ''of excellent families of Cos'' pine for the light: ''O sweet Aurora, you for whom we sang,

in lamplight, the myths of the demigods!'' Perhaps, in fact, the songs on everyone's lips had a myth as their subject: in Horace (*Odes* 1.17.20) the beautiful Tyndaris will sing in private to Horace, *Penelopen vitreamque Circen.*

57. Sextus Empiricus, *Pyrrhonean Outlines* 1.147.

58. For little girls followed the teachings of the grammarian but stopped before reaching the rule of the rhetorician; I add that classes were ''coeducational'': little girls and boys sat side by side listening to the grammarian. This detail, which seems little known, is found in Martial 8.3.15 and 9.68.2, and in Soranus, *On the Maladies of Women,* chap. 92 (p. 209 Dietz); cf. Friedländer, *Sittengeschichte Roms,* 9th ed. (Leipzig: Hirzel, 1919), vol. 1, p. 409. Mythology was learned in school.

59. On Lamias and other Greek boogeymen, see, above all, Strabo 1.8. C. 19, in a chapter that is also important for the study of attitudes toward myth. On Amor and Psyche, see O. Weinreich, *Das Märchen von Amor und Psyche und andere Volksmärchen im Altertum,* in the ninth edition of Freidländer's *Sittengeschichte Roms,* vol. 4, p. 89.

60. So poor that, although not living under autarchy, he does not know the use of money and barters his wine and wheat for a steer or a ram (1.129.7 Kayser). This is plausible; see J. Crawford in *Journal of Roman Studies* 60 (1970) on the rarity of monetary finds in nonurban sites.

61. *Heroicus* 9.141.6. At the springs of Clitumne, the walls and columns of the temple were covered with graffiti, ''which celebrated the god'' (Pliny, *Letters* 8.8). Cf., in Mitteis-Wilcken, *Chrestomathie d. Papyruskunde* (Hildesheim: Olms, 1963), a letter from a certain Nearchus (number 117). The existence of similar ''proscynean'' graffiti in Egypt is known (for example, on the stones of a temple in Talmis: A. D. Nock, *Essays* [Oxford: Clarendon Press, 1972], p. 358). The first fragment of the *Priapeia* (of which there is also an epigraphic copy [*Corpus inscr. lat.* 5.2803], unless this is not the original) alludes to it: ''For the little that these lines I write here, in leisure, on the walls of your temple are worth, take them in good part, I pray you, (O Priapus).''

62. On the ''quarrel of the ghosts'' in the second century, see Pliny, *Letters* 7.27; Lucian, *Philopseudes;* Plutarch, preface of the *Life of Dion.*

63. On these songs, see note 56, *ad finem.* Also, Euripides, *Ion* 507.

64. Aristotle, *Poetics* 9.8. W. Jaeger, *Paideia* (Paris: Gallimard, 1964), vol. 1, p. 326.

65. This is the idea Trimalchio has about it (Petronius 39.3–4; 48.7; 52.1–2).

66. E. Rohde, *Der griech. Roman* (Berlin, 1876), pp. 24 and 99.

67. Nilsson, *Geschichte der griech. Religion,* vol. 2, p. 58.

68. Polybius 12.24.5.

69. Diodorus 1.3.

70. Diodorus 3.61; books 4 and 6 are devoted to the heroic and divine generations of Greece. The Trojan War doubtless figured in book 7. These first books of Diodorus, with their geographic scope and the enormous role given to the mythical, perhaps give an idea of what the first books of Timaeus were like.

71. In 5.41–46 and in a fragment of book 6, preserved by Eusebius (*Evangelical Preparation* 2.59). H. Dörrie, ''Der Königskult des Antiochos von Kommagene,'' *Abhandl. Akad. Göttingen* 3, 60 (1964): 218, considers that the novel of Euhemerus was

a political utopia and mirror for princes. It provided the model or justification for the king as public benefactor. Perhaps. However, the portion accorded to the marvelous and the picturesque far surpasses the political allusions; moreover, not the whole island of Panchaia obeys a king; there is also a city, a kind of priestly republic. In fact, the idea that the gods are worthy men who have been divinized or taken for gods is everywhere and extends far beyond the work of Euhemerus, who confined himself to utilizing it to write a tale.

72. Strabo 1.2.35, p. 43 C.

73. Diodorus 4.1.1.

74. Diodorus 4.8. In the *Evangelical Preparation,* book 2, Eusebius quotes at length the mythographies of Diodorus on Cadmus and Heracles.

75. Around 1873, the young philologist Nietzsche wrote, "With what poetic liberty did not the Greeks treat their gods! We have got too much into the habit of opposing truth and nontruth in history; when one thinks that it is absolutely necessary for Christian myths to be accepted as historically authentic . . . ! Man demands the truth and makes a gift of it *[leistet sie]* in ethical commerce with other men; all collective life rests on this; one anticipates the dire effects of reciprocal lies. Out of this is born the duty to tell the truth. But lies are permitted to the epic narrator because there no harmful consequence is to be feared. Thus lies are permitted where they procure pleasure: the beauty and grace of the lie, but on the condition that it does no harm! It is in this fashion that the priest invents the myths of his gods; the lie serves to prove that the gods are sublime. We have the greatest difficulty in reviving the mythical feeling of the freedom to lie; the great Greek philosophers still lived entirely within this right to lie *[Berechtigung zur Lüge].* The quest for the truth is an acquisition that humanity has made with extreme slowness" (*Philosophenbuch,* 44 and 70, in vol. 10 of the Kröner edition). [English based on the author's retranslation of the text.—Trans.]

76. Dio Cassius (74.18), finding himself in Asia, was in 221 A.D. the nearby witness of the following event, in which he believed without reservation: "A *daimon* who said he was the famous Alexander of Macedonia, who bore a facial resemblance to him and was fitted out like him, came forth from the Danubian regions, where he appeared I don't know how; he crossed the (Moesia?) and Thrace, acting like Dionysus, with four hundred men, bearing the thyrsus and a *nebris,* and who harmed no one." The crowds gathered, with governors and the procurators at the fore; "he moved [or: they followed him in procession] as far as Byzantium by day, just as he had announced; then he left this city for Chalcedonia; there he performed nocturnal rites, buried a wooden horse beneath the earth, and disappeared."

77. Plautus, *Mercator* 487, commented on by Ed. Fraenkel, *Elementi plautini in Plauto* (Florence: La Nuova Italia, 1960), p. 74. For Sextus Empiricus, Artermidorus, and Pausanias, see notes 57, 134 and 22.

78. See note 24; Cicero, *Tusculan Disputations* 1.41.98.

79. Varro, quoted by Censorinus, *De die natali* 21 (Jahn, p. 62).

80. Cicero, *De natura deorum* 3.5.11. Similarly, in the *Art of Love* (1.637) Ovid admits that he believes in the gods only with hesitancy and reserve (cf. Hermann Fränkel, *Ovid, ein Dichter zwischen zwei Welten* [Darmstadt: Wiss. Buchg., 1974], p. 98 and n. 65, p. 194). Philemon had written, "Have gods and make a cult unto them,

but do not make any inquiries on the subject; your seeking will bring you no further; do not wish to know if they exist or not; worship them as if they existed and were very near'' (fragment 118A–B Kock, in Stobaeus 2.1.5). Cf. Aristophanes, *The Knights* 32. For the friendship between Theseus and Pirithous as a *fabula ficta*, see *De finibus* 1.20.64.

81. Cicero, *De re publica* 2.2.4 and 10.18. The historicity of Romulus was accepted well into the nineteenth century, but for different reasons from those of Cicero, as we will see. Cicero believes in Romulus as the founder of Rome because the myth contains a historic kernel (there is no smoke without fire), and history is the politics of the past; Bossuet believes in Romulus and Hercules out of respect for the texts, which he has trouble distinguishing from reality.

82. Menander the Rhetorician, *On the Discourses of the Apparatus* (*Rhetores Graeci,* vol. 3, p. 359, [9, Spengel]).

83. Isocrates, *Demonikos* 50.

84. Diodorus 4.1.2.

85. See, for example, *Politics* 1284A: ''The myth that is told about the Argonauts abandoning Heracles''; *Nicomachean Ethics* 1179a25: ''If the gods take any interest in human affairs, as is believed. . . .'' Aristotle did not believe any of it; the god-stars are prime movers, not providences.

86. See notes 4 and 23; for Palaephatus (chap. 2), the Minotaur was a handsome young man, named Taurus, whom Pasiphaë fell in love with; Thucydides does not doubt the existence of Cecrops or Theseus, either (2.15).

87. Thucydides 1.3 and 2.29.

88. Thucydides 6.2.

89. For the mythic ages in Plato (*Politics* 268E–269B; *Timaeus* 21A–D; *Laws* 677D–685E), who rectifies them and believes in them no more nor less than Thucydides and Pausanias, see Raymond Weil, *L'Archéologie de Platon* (Paris: Klincksieck, 1959), pp. 14, 30, 44.

90. Strabo 1.2.38, C. 45; 40, C. 46; 1.3.2, C. 48.

91. Lucretius, *De natura rerum* 5.324.

92. Polybius 2.41.4, 4.59.5, 34.4.

93. We will cite, in order: Galen, *De optima secta, ad Thrasybulum* 3 (*Opera*, vol. 1, p. 110 Kühn); *De placitis Hippocratis et Platonis* 3.8 (5.357 Kühn; for the expression ''reduce legend to verisimilitude,'' see Plato *Phaedrus*, 229E, which Galen transcribes almost verbatim); *De usu partium* 3.1 (3.169 Kühn; 1.123 Helmreich); *Isagoge seu Medicus* 1 (14.675 Kühn). Note that here Galen mentions Asclepius in a rhetorical vein, but at the same time he had made a private devotion to him (vol. 19, p. 19 Kühn), the sincerity of which the example of his contemporary and equal in devotion, Aelius Aristides, forbids one to suspect. This did not prevent the same Galen from having a demythologized idea of the gods; like many of the learned, he thought that Greek polytheism was the popular deformation of the true knowledge of the gods, who are nothing other, literally, than stars, which are considered as so many living beings, in the ordinary meaning of the word, but endowed with faculties that are more perfect than those of men. For the surprising pages that this anatomist wrote on the perfection of these divine bodies, see *De usu partium corporis humani* 17.1 (vol. 4, pp. 358 ff. Kühn; cf. ibid., 3.10, vol. 3, p. 238 Kühn).

5. Behind This Sociology an Implicit Program of Truth

94. Pausanias 7.2.6–7.

95. On the mythmaking function, see the admirable second chapter of *Deux sources de la morale et de la religion* (Paris: Presses Universitaires de France, 1932), pp. 111, 124, 204.

96. Fontenelle, *De l'origine des fables,* in *Oeuvres diverses* (Amsterdam, 1742), pp. 481–500. Fontenelle's conception remains completely original and resembles neither Voltaire's ideas nor those of the twentieth century. For Fontenelle, myth speaks of nothing and for nothing. Indeed, in his view, myth conceals no truth, but the imaginative function does not exist, either. Everything is explained by the fatal encounter of numerous tiny, innocent faults: ignorance, enthusiasm, a taste for dressing up the anecdote, the author's vanity, worthy curiosity, etc. There are not two sides, tricksters and the naïve; all men are their own dupes. Man is made of small "failings." There are no great essences.

97. The word appears first in Herodotus 1.60 and 2.45 and then in Strabo and Pausanias 9.31.7, 8.29.3, and 8.8.3. It is also found in Dionysius of Halicarnassus.

98. Strabo 1.1.8 C. 6.

99. The word appears first in Thucydides (1.21) and then in Strabo, quoted in the preceding note, and Plutarch, cited in note 3, above, and Philostratus (note 124). Add Isocrates, *Panegyricus* 28. For Menander the Rhetorician, the *mythōdes* [i.e., the domain of the legendary, the fabulous] is opposed to ordinary human history, which is "more believable" (p. 359, 9, Spengel).

100. Cicero, *De re publica* 2.10.18: "minus eruditis hominum saeculis, ut fingendi proclivis esset ratio, cum imperiti facile ad credendum impellerentur."

101. Seneca, *De constantia sapientis* 2.2.

102. Thucydides 1.21.1. In opposition to Isocrates (*Paneg.*, 30): the more people there are who affirm a tradition through the ages, the more this secular consent proves its truth.

103. Origen, *Contra Celsum* 1.42 (*Patrologia Graeca* 11.738); Origen adds, "To be fair, without letting oneself be fooled nonetheless, it is necessary when reading history books to discriminate between authentic events, to which we adhere; those in which we must discern a secret allegorical meaning and which are figurative; and, lastly, events unworthy of belief, which were written to procure some pleasure" (the text here is questionable; others read: "which have been written to flatter certain people"). On the ancient problem of history and empiricism, see the remarkable pages of Galen, *De optima secta, ad Thrasybulum,* chapters 14–15 (1.149 Kühn). On the historicity of the Trojan War, we share Finley's skepticism, expressed in *Journal of Hellenic Studies* (1964): 1–9.

104. G. Granger, *La Théorie aristotélicienne de la science* (Paris: Armand Colin, 1976), p. 374.

105. Plato, *Republic* 377D.

106. *Republic* 378D and 382D. On figurative and allegorical meaning, cf. Origen, quoted in note 103. Xenophanes was already protesting against the indignities attributed to the gods. See also Isocrates, *Busiris* 38.

107. *Phaedo* 61B. These poetic myths can tell the truth (*Phaedrus* 259C–D; *Laws* 682A).

108. Strabo 1.1.10 C. 6–7; 1.2.3 C. 15. Let us also cite this astonishing passage from Aristotle's *Metaphysics* (1074b1): "A tradition, come down from the farthest antiquity and transmitted in the form of a myth to the following centuries, informs us that the stars are gods . . . ; all the rest of this tradition was added later, in mythical form, with the aim of persuading the multitude and to serve common interests and laws; thus, gods are given human form . . . ; if we separate the initial foundation from the story and examine it alone . . . , then we will note that this is a truly divine tradition; while according to all verisimilitude, the different arts and philosophies were developed as fully as possible on several occasions and were lost each time, these opinions are, so to speak, the relics of ancient wisdom maintained up to our day" (French trans. by Tricot). The astral religion of the Greek thinkers, so surprising to us, has been excellently depicted by P. Aubenque, *Le Problème de l'Etre chez Aristote* (Paris: Presses Universitaires de France, 1962), pp. 335 ff.

109. See note 98. Aristotle belonged to the first school and detested allegory: "It is not worth subjecting mythical subtleties to serious scrutiny" (*Metaphysics* B 4, 1000a19).

110. Galen, *De placitis Hippocratis et Platonis* 2.3 (vol. 5, p. 225 Kühn), taking account of the context.

111. *De placitis* 2.3 (p. 222 Kühn), for the *Second Analytics*. For the syllogism and logic of Chrysippus, see p. 224, where Galen opposes scientific demonstration to dialectic, with its topics; to rhetoric, with its places; and to sophistic, with its specious word games. Galen considers himself a rigorous mind, eager for apodeictics (*De libris propriis* 11 [vol. 19, p. 39 Kühn]), and, in medicine, he prefers "grammatical," i.e., geometric, "demonstrations" to "rhetorical *pisteis*" (*De foetuum formatione* 6 [vol. 4, p. 695 Kühn]); it would happen that the rhetoricians themselves would feign resorting to scientific demonstration (*De praenotione ad Epigenem* 1 [vol. 14, p. 605]). In the distinction that I am making here between rigor and eloquence, I am describing two attitudes: I am not taking what the philosophical schools called demonstration, dialectic, and rhetoric in the ancient sense or with the same precision; rhetoric employed syllogisms or at least enthymemes, and demonstration, whether consciously or not, was often more dialectical and even rhetorical than demonstrative (see P. Hadot, "Philosophie, dialectique, rhétorique dans l'Antiquité," *Studia philosophica* 39 [1980]: 145). Here we are examining methods of persuasion less than the attitudes toward persuasion and truth; in this respect it is interesting to see Galen reject certain means of persuasion. He does not want to believe without proof, "as one believes in the laws of Moses and Christ" (*De pulsuum differentiis*, vol. 8, pp. 579 and 657). It is no less interesting to see that, among the Stoics, "objective conditions of persuasion blend with a strong subjective conviction" (E. Bréhier, *Chrysippe et l'ancien Stoïcisme* [Paris: Presses Universitaires de France, 1951], p. 63).

112. *De placitis* 6.8 (vol. 5, p. 583 Kühn). On the citations of famous poets, from Homer to Euripides, that Chrysippus multiplied in a wish to prove that the *hēgemonikon* was lodged in the heart and not in the head, see *De placitis* 3.2–3 (pp. 293 ff.). According to Galen, Chrysippus imagined that the more poets he quoted as witnesses, the more he would prove, which is nothing but a rhetorician's tactic (3.3, p. 310). How could the Stoics justify resorting to poetry and myths as authorities? By holding them to be expressions of common sense? That is undoubtedly the answer they would have

given: all men draw shared notions from the data provided by the senses, and all believe in the reality of the gods, in the immortality of the soul, etc. (Bréhier, *Chrysippe*, p. 65). In addition to myths and poetry, the etymology of words was another article of evidence of this common sense (on the *etymon*, both as primary meaning and as true meaning of a word, see Galen, vol. 5, pp. 227 and 295). Proverbs, sayings, and figures of speech function equally as proof. But here again we are examining less what the Stoics thought they were doing than what they did unawares. In any case, at least two ideas coexisted for them: on the one hand, men, in all times, have common notions that are truthful; on the other, men, in the beginning, had a greater and more divine knowledge of truth than do the men of today. Both of these ideas, which are ill matched, attempt in their fashion to justify this mysterious authority that the Stoics attributed to mythical, poetic, and etymological speech. On poetry as having the gift of speaking the truth, see, especially, Plato, *Laws* 682A. Poetry is thus inspired, and every inspired text (for example, that of Plato) will be akin to poetry, even if it is in prose (811C). If poetry is akin to myth, this is not because poets narrate myths but because myth and poetry are both inevitably true and, it can be said, divinely inspired. We understand, then, the real reason why Epicurus condemned poetry: he was not condemning the act of writing verse rather than prose or even, specifically, the mythical (and, in his eyes, false) *content* of many poems; he was condemning poetry as an *authority*, as a so-called source of truth, and he condemned it *in the same way* and on the same level as he condemned myth. He also condemned another mode of so-called persuasion of which we have also spoken: rhetoric.

113. This superstition concerning Homer and poetry in general would be worthy of a study all its own. It will endure until the end of Antiquity. At the beginning of the fifth century there will be a similar division on the subject of Virgil: one group considered him merely a poet, an author of fictions, while others saw in him a fount of knowledge, whose least line spoke the truth and deserved profound examination. See Macrobius, *Saturnalia* 1.24, and 3–5. Here it is another matter: the supposed relations between a text and its referent. On the truth of poetry among the Stoics, the findings of M. Pohlenz, *Die Stoa* (Göttingen: Vandenhoeck & Ruprecht, 1978), are less pertinent than the rest of the book.

114. Galen, *De placitis* 5.7 (vol. 5, p. 490 Kühn). On Chrysippus, Homer, and Galen, see F. Buffière, *Les Mythes d'Homère et la pensée grecque* (Paris: Les Belles Lettres, 1956), p. 274.

115. P. Aubenque, *Le Problème de l'Etre chez Aristote*, p. 100.

116. Aristotle, *Metaphysics* B 4, 1000a12.

117. On myth as ornament or as a pleasant coating to make the truth palatable, see Lucretius 1.935; Aristotle, *Metaphysics* 1074b1; Strabo 1.6.19 C. 27. On the idea that it is impossible to formulate a lie based on nothing, see P. Aubenque, *Le Problème de l'Etre chez Aristote*, p. 72 and note 3.

118. There is so much that could be said on the enormous subject of the allegorical interpretation of myths, and of Homer first of all, that after mentioning the book by Jean Pépin, *Mythe et Allégorie* (Paris: Les Belles Lettres, 1958), and recalling that it was well before the Stoics that this type of interpretation became popularly accepted (Diodorus 3.62: with the physical interpretation of Dionysus forming its basis; cf. Artemidorus, *The Interpretation of Dreams* 2.37 [p. 169 Pack]; and 4.47 [pp. 274, 21]) and that it will

lead into biblical allegorism, we will confine ourselves to citing *On the Cave of the Nymphs*, by Porphyry, the *Homeric Allegories*, by Heraclitus, the *Summary of Theology*, by Cornutus, and to referring the reader to F. Cumont, *Recherches sur le symbolisme funéraire* (Paris: Geuthner, 1942), pp. 2 ff.; F. Buffière, *Les Mythes d'Homère et la pensée grecque* (Paris: Les Belles Lettres, 1956); and P. Decharme, *La Critique des traditions religieuses chez les Grecs, des origines à Plutarque* (Paris, 1905).

119. Plutarch, *De Iside* 20.358F. Plotinus will develop a very similar idea (*Enneads* 3.5.9, 24).

120. Machiavelli, *The Prince*, chap. 61; *Discourse on Livy*, 3.30; see also *Contra Apion*, by Flavius Josephus, 157 ff. (note the idea in chapter 160 that religion enabled Moses to make the people tractable).

121. The only edition of Palaephatus that I had at my disposal dates from 1689 and is found in the *Opuscula mythologica, physica et ethica*, published in Amsterdam by Th. Gale. On Palaephatus, cf. Nestle, *Vom Mythos zum Logos*, p. 149; K. E. Müller, *Geschichte der antiken Ethnographie*, vol. 1, p. 218; F. Jacoby, *Atthis: The Local Chronicles of Ancient Athens* (Oxford: Oxford University Press, 1949), p. 324, note 37.

122. Plato, *Republic* 382D.

123. Pliny, *Natural History* 11.17.1: "reliqua vetustatis situ obruta"; Thucydides 1.21.1; Diodorus 4.1.1.

6. Restoring Etiological Truth to Myth

124. Philostratus, *Heroicus* 7.9, p. 136 (p. 7, 26 De Lannoy).

125. Cicero, *De natura deorum* 3.16.40. See also his *De divinatione* 2.57.117.

126. Philostratus, *Heroicus* 7.9, p. 136 (p. 7, 29 De Lannoy).

127. Pausanias 1.30.3.

128. Pausanias 3.25.5.

129. Artemidorus, *The Interpretation of Dreams* 2.44 (p. 178, 7); 4.47 (p. 272, 16 Pack).

130. Lucretius 5.878, 4.730.

131. Plato, *Republic* 378C; Cicero, *De natura deorum* 2.28.70; Pausanias 8.29.3; Artemidorus, *Interpretation of Dreams* 4.47 (p. 274, 16 Pack); *Aetna* 29–93.

132. I have listed these references in *Pain et Cirque*, p. 581 and note 102, p. 741; above all, let us cite Xenophon, *Memorabilia* 4.3.13.

133. Pausanias 8.2.4–5.

134. Artemidorus 4.47 (p. 274, 2–21 Pack); it goes without saying that I am looking at Festugière's admirable translation; three of my students, Mssrs. Maurice Blanc, Gilbert Casimiri, and Jacques Cheilan, translated Artemidorus with me in 1968, but . . . at any rate we were not able to equal the work of the above translator!

135. Dion of Prusa 11, *Trojan Discourse* 42; Quintilian, *Institutio oratoria* 12.4.

136. Cicero, *De re publica* 2.10.18; Livy, preface, 7; in 1.4.2 he writes that the Vestal attributed the twins' paternity to Mars, "either because she truly believed it, or to conceal her guilt behind an illustrious paternity." Pausanias 9.30.4; in 9.37.7 he again writes, with revealing precision, "the kings Ascalaphus and Ialmenus, *said to be* the sons of Ares and Astyoche, *daughter* of Azeus."

137. Cicero, *De natura deorum* 3.16.40 ff.

138. Cicero, *Tusculan Disputations* 1.12.27 ff.

139. Pausanias 9.2.3–4.

140. Pausanias 9.20.4 and 9.21.1. In 8.46.5 the Greek used by Pausanias (οἱ ἐπὶ τοῖς θαύμασιν) must, I believe, refer to a *procurator a mirabilibus*, or a *minister a mirabilibus*, or some other equivalent title. On the *thaumata* consulted in Rome, see, again, Pausanias 9.21.1; I do not recall that this function has been proved epigraphically.

141. Pausanias 8.22.4. The same reasoning is found in 1.24.1. Was the Minotaur a man, and is he a monster only in legend (cf. note 23)? This is not certain, for one often sees women give birth to monsters.

142. Saint Augustine will say it again in order to explain Methuselah's long life (*City of God* 15.9).

143. Pausanias speaks of this Cleon of Magnesia in 10.4.6.

144. Pausanias 9.18.3–4.

145. Pausanias 4.32.4.

146. Thucydides 2.17.

147. Pausanias 1.38.7 and 4.33.5. These dreams forbade him to reveal certain sacred mysteries. There is nothing more frequent among the literary tribe of the day than obedience to dreams. Artemidorus received the order to write his *Interpretation of Dreams* from Apollo in a dream (*Oneir.* 2, preface, *ad finem*); Dio Cassius received the order to write his *Roman History* from the gods in a dream (23.2); Galen studied medicine as the result of dreams of his father, who saw his son as a doctor (vol. 10, 609 and 16, 223 Kühn); he also obtained the recipe for a medicine from a dream (16, 222).

148. Pausanias 1.28.7.

149. L. Radermacher, *Mythos und Sage bei den Griechen* (Munich, 1938; reprinted 1962), p. 88. F. Prinz, *Gründungsmythen und Sagenchronologie* (Munich, 1979), does not treat our problem.

150. Aeschylus, *Prometheus Bound* 774 and 853.

151. Diodorus 4.1.1.

152. Examples of the discussion of variations among legends, judged by means of synchronisms, include Pausanias 3.24.10–11, 9.31.9, and 10.17.4. On these legendary chronologies, see W. Kroll, *Studien zum Verständnis*, chap. 3 and page 310. It was claimed that the nomothetes Onomacritus, Thales, Lycurgus, Charondas, and Zaleucus had been disciples of one another. Aristotle objected to this on chronological grounds (*Politics* 1274a28); Livy proves in the same way that Numa Pompilius could not have been the disciple of Pythagorus (1.18.2). See also Dionysius of Halicarnassus, *Antiquities* 2.52. On synchromisms in Greek historiography, see A. D. Momigliano, *Essays in Ancient and Modern Historiography*, p. 192, and *Studies in Historiography*, p. 213.

153. Isocrates, *Busiris* 36–37.

154. Pausanias 8.15.6–7. Pausanias discusses other homonymies in 7.19.9–10 and 7.22.5. It is in order to resolve chronological and prosopographical problems that in the Hellenistic period it was necessary to conclude that several heroes named Heracles, several gods named Dionysus, and even several named Zeus existed (Diodorus, Strabo, and even Cicero say it; cf. Pausanias 9.27.8).

155. On the subject of this first Olympic competition, see Strabo 8.3.30 C. 355 (who on this occasion makes a distinction between Heracles, the son of Alcmene, and the Heracles of the Couretes, and concludes: "All of that is told in several ways and is absolutely not worth believing"); Pausanias 5.4.5, 5.8.5, 8.26.4; on the beginning of the Olympic computation, 6.19.13 and 8.2.2 (in his dating of the synchronisms of the oldest Greek contests, Pausanias refuses to count the first Olympic competition, in which Heracles and Apollo took part). Pausanias knows, moreover, that there was a time when the Eleans did not yet record the names of the victors (6.19.4). On the synchronism between the year 776, King Iphitus, who founded ("refounded") the contest, and Lycurgus, see Pausanias 5.4.5, and Plutarch, *Life of Lycurgus* 1.

156. On this date, see Timaeus, cited by Censorinus, *De die natali* 21.3. On the relationship between mythical and historical time, see, for example, Pausanias 8.1–5 and 6.

157. Pausanias 7.18.5; another example can be found in 7.4.1.

158. Athenaeus 1.16F–17B (*Odyssey* 1.107).

159. Cf. note 14. Pausanias quotes, for example, a certain Callipus of Corinth, the author of a history of Orchomenus (11.29.2 and 38.10). He says that he questions "the locals," "the people" (8.41.5), who sometimes do not know; then he speaks to "those of the indigenous population to whom the old historical books (*hypomnēmata*) have been transmitted." Another time, only the old man of the village knows the origin of a custom (8.42.13 and 6.24.9). Among his informants are a *nomophylax* of Elis (6.23.6), the Thyiades of Athens (10.4.3), his host in Larissa (9.23.6), and an Ephesian (5.5.9). See, however, F. Jacoby, *Atthis: The Local Chronicles of Ancient Athens*, p. 237, note 2, and the appendix, p. 399.

160. Pausanias 9.1.2. On all these questions of genealogy and etiology, see the *Atthis* of F. Jacoby, particularly pp. 143 ff. and 218 ff. The political importance of local mythical history is confirmed by epigraphy (the Parian Marble, the list of the priests of Poseidon in Halicarnassus, the Lindus Chronicle).

161. Pausanias 7.1–2.

162. Pausanias 9.9.

163. We know that, from the classical period onward, kinship among cities was a diplomatic argument (see for example, Herodotus 7.150; Xenophon, *Hellenica* 6.3.6). For Lanuvium and Centuripes, see J. and L. Robert, "Bulletin épigraphique," *Revue des études grecques* 78 (1965): 197. For Sparta and Jerusalem, see 2 Maccabees, chap. 4. The Etruscans also know the rest of the Trojan legend, and they had Greek mythology as their mythology; this in no way allows us to conclude that they knew a legend about Aeneas as the founder of Rome; on the contrary, this type of invention lies completely in the mainstream of Hellenistic pseudo-history, and I believe, for my part, that J. Perret's thesis is the good one. We know, moreover, that the reading of the name of Aeneas on an archaic cippus in Tor Tignosa is a misreading (*Année épigraphique* [1969–70], no. 2).

164. Jacques de Voragine, author of the *Golden Legend*, also wrote a history of Genoa, his home, in which we learn that this town had as its founder Janus, the first king of Italy, and then, as a second founder, a second Janus, homonym of the first and, like Aeneas, a citizen of Troy. For a long time the history of southern Italian art was falsified by a Neapolitan scholar who in 1743 fabricated a whole series of artists, complete with names, dates, and biography (E. Bertaux, *L'Art dans l'Italie méridionale*, new ed.

[Ecole française de Rome, 1980], preface). I imagine that this "forger" wished to give the South its own Vasari.

165. "On Epideictic Discourse," in *Rhetores Graeci*, vol. 3, p. 356, 30, Spengel.

7. Myth and Rhetorical Truth

166. See note 75. On this point, we are pleased also to cite Paul Feyerabend's original and courageous book, *Contre la méthode: Esquisse d'une théorie anarchiste de la connaissance*, French trans. (Paris: Seuil, 1979), p. 302 and note 1, on lies and fiction in archaic Greece.

167. Herodotus 9.26–28. The role of Athens in the war of the Amazons is likewise exalted in the *Epitaphios* of Lysias (2.3 ff.). Cf. Y. Thébert, "L'image du Barbare à Athènes," *Diogène* 112 (1980): 100.

168. In diplomatic matters the use of myth bridges the possible gap between interests at stake and commitments already made. The Jews state to the Spartans, who are careful not to question it, that their two peoples are brothers by Abraham; the fraternity thus sealed rarely had to be tested, and so it was necessary from time to time to renew the formalities (1 Maccabees, chap. 12). From time to time it was useful, and the vanquished high priest Jason will go to Sparta to end his days. Cf. B. Cardauns, "Juden und Spartaner," *Hermes* 95 (1967): 314. When, on the contrary, an alliance or reversal of alliances is founded on living and present interests, there is no reason to invoke the legendary kinship, and it would even be ridiculous to do so; this is quite evident in Xenophon's *Hellenica* 6.3, where the pompous and ridiculous speech of Callias is set in opposition to that of the other Athenian deputies.

169. Cf. an amusing passage from the *Hippias major*, 285D–E. This mode of praise reached its apex in the imperial period. Apuleius pronounced the eulogy of Carthage several times (*Florida* 18 and 20); Favorinus gave that of Corinth (this panegyric was given in the name of Dion of Prusa and forms his 37th *Discourse*); and Tertullian gave praise to his Carthaginian compatriots. In all these cases it will be noted that Carthage and Corinth, both Roman colonies, are considered to be ancient cities; Corinth is supposed to continue the old Greek city, which had been destroyed by the Romans more than two centuries earlier and replaced by a colony bearing the same name; Carthage is likewise supposed to continue the city of Dido and Hannibal. Here we see the operation of etiological thought, which erases history and individualizes by means of origins.

170. Plato, *Menexenus* 235A–B.

171. Aristophanes, *The Archarnians* 636 (cf. *The Knights* 1329); Herodas 2.95.

172. Xenophon, *Hellenica* 6.3 (cf. note 168).

173. It is in this way that Pausanias (cited note 133), and Saint Augustine (*Confessions* 6.6) are ironic concerning another type of panegyric, that addressed to the emperors. "My lies as a panegyrist were sure to obtain the approval of the listeners, who, however, knew the truth," writes Saint Augustine.

174. Isocrates, *Panegyric of Athens* 54 (cf. 68) and 28.

8. Pausanias Entrapped

175. Pausanias 2.21.5; see also 1.26.6 and 7.18.7, 4. Another "rationalist" interpretation of a myth will be found in 5.1.4: instead of being Luna's lover, Endymion had children by a princess he married, and their sons are the eponyms of the Aetolians

and the Paeonians. For Pausanias that is history; for, as a disciple of Thucydides, he believes in the royalties of the heroic days and in eponymous ancestors. In 2.21.1 Pausanias refuses to discuss the matter. See also 2.17.4.

176. Pausanias 8.10.9; the same mood can be found in 8.10.4, 5.13.6, and 6.26.2. On this last text, see R. Demangel in *Revue internationale des droits de l'Antiquité* 2 (1949): 226, who asks himself "the question of good faith in ancient devotion" and admits that pious and therefore sincere mystifications can exist there.

177. Pausanias 6.26.2.

178. Pausanias 8.8.3.

179. Pausanias 8.3.6; at this point the Greeks tell a myth about Zeus as Callisto's lover, which is unworthy of the majesty of the gods; it is no less childish and mythological to believe that the gods transform their lovers into stars.

180. H. W. Pleket, "Zur Soziologie des antiken Sports," in *Mededelingen van het Nederlands Instituut te Rome* 36 (1974): 57. In the middle of the imperial era, athletes often were recruited from the elite classes (cf. F. Millar's study on Dexippus in the *Journal of Roman Studies* [1969]), and this is why athletic sports are not relegated to the so-called popular culture. When the Cynics or Dion of Prusa make ironic comments about athletic contests in their diatribes, they find fault with madness and men's vain passions or else the Greeks in general; they are not showing disdain for a diversion that is good only for the lesser classes. Things were completely different in Rome, where, as G. Ville shows in his great book, *La Gladiature* (Ecole française de Rome, 1982), spectacles were considered to be good for the populace. Cicero and Pliny the Younger did attend them, but they affected a certain disdain. But, precisely, at Rome the actors in the spectacles, far from being recruited from good society, were, as Ville indicates, the meanest of buffoons. In other respects, Pausanias had a "glorifying" attitude toward the Greek past that was common in his time; see E. L. Bowi, "Greeks and Their Past in the Second Sophistic," *Past and Present* 46 (1970): 23.

181. I am being specific, for it happens that Pausanias speaks in his own name when he states that one version is preferable to another; in 9.20.4 he opposes the correct explanation of the tritons to the mythical one (see note 140); in 8.39.2 Pausanias does not say why it is better to believe that Phigalus is the son of Lycaon rather than an autochthonous figure. The only explanation is that Pausanias believes in the genealogy of the kings of Arcadia (cf. 8.3.1). Furthermore, he deliberately states that he believes in the historicity of Lycaon (8.2.4). Arcadia, as we know, was his road to Damascus.

182. Pausanias 8.14.5–8; another example can be found in 8.12.9.

183. Pausanias 9.31.7–9.

184. We refer the reader to the classic study by L. C. Knights, *Explorations* (London, 1946): "How Many Children Had Lady Macbeth?"; cf. R. Wellek and A. Warren, *Theory of Literature* (Fr. trans. [Paris: Seuil, 1971]), p. 35.

185. Pausanias 8.3.6–7; cf. note 179. Still playing the philological game of internal consistency, Pausanias infers elsewhere that the "race of the Sileni" is mortal since tombs of a Silenus are shown in different places (6.24.8); it goes without saying that Pausanias does not believe in the Sileni any more than the contemporaries of Carneades believed in nymphs, Pans, and Satyrs (Cicero *De natura deorum* 3.17.43).

186. Cicero denies oracles just as he denies "natural divination" (*De divinatione*

2.56.115). Oenomaus can be read in book 2 of the *Evangelical Preparation* by Eusebius; cf. P. Vallette, *De Oenomao Cynico* (Paris, 1908); Diogenianus can be read in books 2 and 5 of Eusebius. Plotinus, on the contrary, believes in oracles (*Enneads* 2.9.9.41).

187. In 8.10.9 Pausanias seriously questions the matter of divine intervention in a war and invokes the indisputable precedent of the Delphic oracle, which was protected by a miracle; indeed, the Galatians were frightened by a storm, an earthquake, and a collective panic (Pausanias 10.23). On the divine "epiphanies" that protect a temple, see P. Roussel, "Un miracle de Zeus Panamaros," *Bulletin de correspondance hellénique* 55 (1931): 70, and the fourth section of the Chronicle of Lindus.

188. Pausanias 8.8.3; cf. note 19.

189. Pausanias 7.23.7–8.

190. Pausanias 8.8.3.

191. For Sallustius, *De diis et mundo* 4, for example, in the physicians' meaning Cronos is Chronos, Time, who devours its own moments; in the theologians' interpretation, Cronos, devouring his own children, is an "enigma" that means that Intelligence is confused with the Intelligible, i.e., with its own object; for Plotinus, already, Cronos was Intelligence. On occasion, Pausanias could have heard the middle Platonists or the Stoics, both great allegorists.

192. Pausanias 8.2.3–4.

193. Lucretius 5.1170. Few ideas could be more foreign to Neoplatonism, which ignores historicity.

194. Pausanias 8.2.6–7. On Arcadia as the conservatory of the most ancient civilization, let us recall that Callimachus had written an *Arcadia* and that he set the scene of his Hymn to Zeus there. People were struck by the Arcadians' piety (Polybius 4.20) and their virtuous poverty. In Arcadia, free citizens, heads of families, were reduced to working with their own hands instead of commanding servants (Polybius 4.21). The Arcadians lived on acorns, the first food of humanity, longer than all the other Greeks (Galen, vol. 6, p. 621 Kühn). The theme is a revealing one. The Arcadians are not a backward people; they have maintained an ancient state that has remained intact and unchanged. That Arcadian traditions are very ancient does not mean that they go back to a more distant past than others; it means, rather, that their traditions lead one back without any change to a past the memory of which, among other peoples, has been corrupted and suffered interpolations. In other words, the Arcadian traditions transmit to us an authentic state. The two ideas of Pausanias are that the past conveyed by tradition is too often gradually encrusted with false legends (but such was not the case in Arcadia), and also that the past may be reconstituted on the basis of the traces of it that remain in the present. The past is found in the present; this already was the principle that Thucydides had applied in his Archeology.

195. Pausanias 8.35.8; this Pamphos is older than Homer (8.37.9) and only Olen is more ancient than he (9.27.2). It should be known that Pausanias had made special inquiries on the period when Homer lived, but he abandoned the idea of publishing his conclusions because of the dogmatism prevalent among the specialists on Homeric poetry (9.30.3).

196. Pausanias 8.29.1–4. For Xenophanes, see note 50.

197. Pausanias 9.40.11–41, 5.

198. See note 152; I will not develop it here, for fear of wearying the reader.

199. Pausanias 9.1.1–2.

9. Forger's Truth, Philologist's Truth

200. A. D. Momigliano has recalled that this classic phrase of Ranke's acutally comes from Lucian, *How To Write History*, p. 39.

201. A. Boeckh, *Enzyklopädie und Methodenlehre der philologischen Wissenschaften*, vol. 1: *Formale Theorie der philol. Wiss.* (1877; reprinted. Darmstadt: Wiss. Buch., 1967).

202. M. Riffaterre, *La Production du texte* (Paris. Seuil, 1979), p. 176: "Philology's entire effort was to reconstitute vanished realities, out of fear that the poem would die with its referent."

203. Strabo 8.8.2 C. 388. More generally, let us quote Strabo 8.8.3 C. 337: "I compare the current state of places with what Homer says. One has to, the poet is so famous and familiar to us. My readers will think that I have attained my end only if nothing in there contradicts what the poet in whom everyone has such great confidence says on his part."

204. P. Hadot, "Philosophie, exégèse et contresens," *Actes du XIVᵉ Congrès international de philosophie* (Vienna, 1968): 335–37.

205. The anecdote is found in Quintilian 1.8.21. On this general matter, see M. Foucault, *Les Mots et les choses* (Paris: Gallimard, 1966), pp. 55 and 141, on the sciences in the sixteenth century: "The great tripartition, so simple in appearance, of observation, evidence, and myth, did not exist. . . . When one has the history of an animal to consider, it is useless and impossible to choose between the word of the naturalist and that of the compiler. It is necessary to put into one and the same form of knowledge everything that has been seen and heard, everything that has been said." To be brief, we will limit ourselves to referring the reader to Quintilian, *Inst. orat.* 1.8.18–21.

206. A. Puech, *Histoire de la littérature grecque chrétienne* (Paris: Les Belles Lettres, 1930), vol. 3, p. 181: "General history appeared in the works of Eusebius only through and by means of literary history." Puech understands literary history in the old sense of the term: history told through the literature that transmits its memory.

207. Pliny, *Natural History* 7.56 (57), 191. Another list of inventors is found in Clement of Alexandria, *Stromateis* 1.74: Atlas invented navigation, the Dactyls, iron, Apis, medicine, and Medea, dye for hair; but Ceres and Bacchus have disappeared from the list . . . Bacchus, who was only a man, precedes Heracles by sixty-three years, according to Clement, a great chronologist. Bacchus receives no credit for an invention. Pliny and Clement were brought to this point by a scheme, an instrument of reason, the questionnaire: Who invented what? For the questionnaire was one of the mental techniques of the time (there were others—for example, the lists of excellences: the Seven Wonders of the World, the Twelve Great Orators . . .). As J.-C. Passeron has recently written, "Lists and tables, maps and classifications, concepts and diagrams, are not the pure and simple transcriptions of the utterances that predated them, but under the constraints of graphic logic they cause assertions, parallels, and additions to appear" ("Les Yeux et les oreilles," forward to *L'Oeil à la page*, G.I.D.E.S. [November, 1979], Paris, p. 11).

208. The reader amused by these details should read Yves-Paul Pezron, *L'Antiquité des tems rétablie et défenduë contre les Juifs et les nouveaux chronologistes* (Paris, 1687), where he will learn that in the year 2538 of the creation of the world Jupiter had three children by Europa. I learned of this author thanks to G. Couton (see note 7). As for Dom Calmet, his universal history, which delighted Voltaire so much, appeared in 1735.

209. Saint Augustine admits it in the *City of God*, in the beginning of chapter 10 of book 2. It was not important. Anti-pagan polemics were more of a brouhaha concerning false gods than a rational mode of persuasion.

210. Indeed, everything seems to start from the beginning. A fine study by F. Hampl, *Geschichte als kritische Wissenschaft* (Darmstadt: Wiss. Buch., 1975), vol. 2, pp. 1–50: "Mythos, Sage, Märchen," shows that it would be useless to distinguish among tale, legend, and myth by attributing a different degree of veracity or a different relationship to religion to each one. "Myth" is not a transhistorical element or an invariant. The genres practiced by mythical thinking are as multiple, variable, and indescribable as the other literary genres practiced throughout the literatures of all peoples and all periods. Myth is not an essence.

10. The Need to Choose between Culture and Belief in a Truth

211. Guy Lardreau, "L'Histoire comme nuit de Walpurgis," *Cahiers de l'Herne: Henry Corbin* (1981): 115, a sober article imbued with an authentic philosophical spirit.

212. Cf. "Foucault révolutionne l'histoire," in Veyne, *Comment on écrit l'histoire*, pp. 203–42 (paperback edition).

213. On the illusion of the absence of limits, see Veyne, *Comment on écrit l'histoire*, p. 216.

214. The words "Man cannot fail to learn" are found in Habermas' *Raison et légitimité* (Paris: Payot, 1978), if my memory serves me well. For the relations of production, see his *Connaissance et intérêt* (Paris: Gallimard, 1974), pp. 61 and 85. The dense criticism of historical materialism made by R. Aron, *Introduction à la philosophie de l'histoire* (Paris: Gallimard, 1938), pp. 246–50, remains fundamental. Aron rightly concludes that this criticism does not refute Marxism itself, which is a philosophy rather than a science of history.

215. F. Jacob, *La Logique du vivant: Une histoire de l'hérédité* (Paris: Gallimard, 1971), p. 22: "Simply to see a body, hitherto invisible, is not enough to transform it into an object of analysis; when Leeuwenhoek looks at a drop of water under a microscope for the first time, he finds an unknown world—a complete, unsuspected animal kingdom that the instrument suddenly makes accessible to observation. But the mind of his time can make nothing of this world. It has no use to propose for these microscopic beings, no relationship that would link them to the rest of the living world; this discovery only enlivens conversations." A similar conception of matter (which, Duns Scotus would have said, is in the act, but without being the act of nothing) explains Nietzsche's famous phrase, often attributed to Max Weber, which has become the touchstone of the problem of historical objectivity: "Facts do not exist." See *Der Wille zur Macht*, no. 70 and 604 Kröner: "Es gibt keine Tatsachen." Nietzsche's influence on Max Weber, which was considerable, would be worthy of a study of its own.

216. Cf. note 210.

Index

Achaea, kings of, 101
Achaeans, 77
Aeneas, 50, 135 n. 32, 136 n. 35
Aeneid, 136 n. 35
Agamemnon, 100
Ages, mythic, 142 n. 89
Aitiai (origins), 25, 123
Akoē (hearsay), 132–33 n. 13
Alexandrianism, 45, 101
Allegory, 25, 29, 143 n. 103, 144 n. 109;
   myth as, 100, 123; Stoic view of, 62,
   65–66
Amazons, 80, 92
Amor, 140 n. 59
Analogy, 26, 88
Ancients and Moderns, Quarrel of, 112
Aniles fabulae, 139 n. 56
Antonines, 24
Apion (grammarian), 76
Apollo, 55, 71, 75, 148 n. 155
Apotheosis, 90. *See also* Divinization
Appian, 54
Aquinas, Thomas, 11
Arcadia, 11, 96, 98–102, 151 n. 194
Archeology (Thucydides), 95, 151 n.
   194
Archetype, 26, 76
Ares, 75
Argos, 77
Aristomenes, 74
Aristophanes, 29, 31, 137 n. 43
Aristotle, 49, 69, 144 n. 109; *Meta-
   physics,* 65, 134 n. 54; on myth, 14,
   52, 57, 65, 67, 133 n. 23, 142 n. 85,

144 n. 108, 147 n. 152; *Poetics,* 45;
   Politics, 124, 131 n. 4
Aron, Raymond, 88, 153 n. 214
Artemidorus, 48, 72–73
Artemis, 73
Asclepius, 55
Atheism, ancient, 113
Athens, 80
Athletes, 150 n. 180
Atreus, 101
Augustan History, 12–13, 133 n. 21
Augustine, Saint, 135 n. 32, 138 nn. 44,
   45, 153 n. 209
Author, notion of, 133 n. 13
Authority, 6, 8, 28, 32, 64, 90

Bacchus, 48
Bad-Tempered Man (Menander), 43
Balkanization, 56, 92
Barbarians, 96
Beaufort, 2, 132 n. 11
Becoming, historical, 36–37
Belief: contradictions in, xi, 54, 56,
   112–13; modalities of, 1, 27–28, 32,
   65, 79, 135 n. 33
Benefactions, 47, 48
Bergson, H., 36, 59, 84, 127
Béroul, 91–92
Boeckh, 109
Bossuet, 1–2, 11, 108, 109, 111, 113,
   142 n. 81
Bourdieu, P., 34, 139 n. 52
Busiris, 75

155